# SAVE THE FAMILY

### THE HETEROSEXUAL

### &

### THE HOMOSEXUAL

Rev. Anthony Martin

25 Time Author-Inspirational/Motivational Speaker

The Kingdom Culture Fellowship Ministries
Christian Self Publishing Co.

Copyright © 2017, 2018 by Rev. Anthony Martin

*SAVE THE FAMILY~THE HETEROSEXUAL & THE HOMOSEXUAL*
By Rev. Anthony Martin

Printed in the United States of America

ISBN 978-1-63273-020-6

All rights reserved solely by the author. The author guarantees all contents are original and do not infringe upon the legal rights of any other person or work. No part of this book may be reproduced in any form without the permission of the author. Unless otherwise indicated, Bible quotations are taken from The Kingdom Culture Exploratory Study Bible. The Kingdom English Standard Bible Edition (TKESB). Copyright © 2015 by The kingdom Culture Fellowship Ministries Christian Self Publishing Co.™ Used by permission. All rights reserved.

www.thekingdomcultureblog.com

Google ~ Rev. Anthony Martin ~

# Contents

Preface.................................................................... iv
Introduction............................................................ v

## Part I: The Heterosexuals

1. The Purpose for Man......................................... 16
2. The Purpose for Woman ................................... 24
3. The Purpose for Sex ........................................... 34
4. Not Born, A Choice ........................................... 51

## Part II: The Homosexuals

5. Civil Rights or Human Rights .......................... 91
6. Sodom and Gomorrah ..................................... 123
7. The Worlds Way ............................................... 166
8. The Rainbow Covenant .................................. 194
9. Queen James Doctrine ................................... 218
A Message to the Christian

But you yourselves wrong and defraud—even your own brothers! Or do you not know that the unrighteous will not inherit the kingdom of God? Do not be deceived: neither the sexually immoral, nor idolaters, nor adulterers, nor men who practice homosexuality, nor thieves, nor the greedy, nor drunkards, nor revilers, nor swindlers will inherit the kingdom of God.
1 Cor. 6:8~10

INTRODUCTION

## *The Battle*

---

The question behind marriage is a structural one that precedes lawmaking. The argument about the structural identity of marriage is not a legal argument about how people should be treated within the bonds of that structure. Rather, it is about whether homosexual relationships should be identified as having the structure of marriage, and only after that can civil rights considerations emerge about how citizens should be treated fairly with respect to marriage. Those who want homosexual relationships to be redefined as marriages say that many aspects of their relationships are like marriage—having sexual play, living together, loving one another, etc.—and therefore they should be allowed to call their relationships marriages and should be recognized in the law as marriage partners. But this cannot be a proper legal matter until the empirical case has been made that a homosexual partnership and a marriage are indistinguishable. Otherwise, the appeal amounts to nothing more than a request that homosexual partners be allowed to call themselves what they want to call themselves regardless of the differences that exist in reality. The answer they want is for law making and adjudicating authorities to change the law based on the principle that reality is defined by the will and declarations of individuals, not as it is thru "GODLY PRINCIPLES", all of whom should be treated without discrimination. But here, you see, is the sleight of hand. The appeal now being made for homosexual marriage rights is not an appeal for judges and lawmakers to reconsider past empirical judgments about similarities and differences between heterosexual and homosexual relationships

# INTRODUCTION

Rather, it is an appeal for judges and lawmakers to ignore those distinctions in order not to deny citizens the right to call things what they want to call them. .It is a version of an appeal for the protection of free speech, and in this case it is a demand that the speech of particular persons carry the authority to define the Homosexual Community without regard to the basis of the GODLY principles that is indoctrinated in the Sealed Constitution of these United States of America. The antidiscrimination principle is appealed not in order to show that some married couples have previously been denied the recognition of their marriage. Rather the antidiscrimination principle is being used to ask that no citizen be denied the right to call something what he or she wants to call it. If homosexual relationships are, in this manner, legally recognized as marriages, no realities will change. Heterosexual marriage partners will still be able to engage in sexual intercourse and potentially procreate children; homosexual partners will still not be able to engage in such intercourse. Pregnancy will still be possible only by implanting a male sperm in a female egg, whether that is done by sexual intercourse inside or outside of marriage, or by in vitro fertilization, or by implanting male sperm in the uterus of a woman not married to the man whose sperm are being used. **The only thing that will change is that the law will mistakenly use the word "marriage" to refer to two different kinds of sexually intimate human relationships men and woman as we see it are highly receiving sex change operation, the implant of breast, the removal of the penis and for the woman the removal of the breast and vagina in place for a penis implant. Hormone injection toward the men that estrogen flow within the man and for the woman testosterone flows thru her, this would be the change.**

# INTRODUCTION

If this happens, we will need to pay close attention to the consequences. Judges and public officials will then be required to recognize as a marriage any sexually Intimate bond between two people who want to call themselves married. This means that there will no longer be any basis for distinguishing legally between a heterosexual union and a homosexual relationship. Which means henceforth that there will be no legal basis for restrictions against a homosexual couples obtaining children in any way they choose for such restrictions would constitute discrimination. And it will mean that when a mature mother and son, or father and daughter, or trio or quartet of partners come to the courts or to the marriage-license bureau to ask that their sexually active relationship be recognized as marriage, there will be no legal grounds *of a non-arbitrary kind* to reject the request **The only thing that will change is that the law will mistakenly use the word "marriage" to refer to two different kinds of sexually intimate human relationships, men and woman as we see it are highly receiving sex change operation, the implant of breast, the removal of the penis and for the woman the removal of the breast and vagina in place for a penis implant. Hormone injection toward the men that estrogen flow within the man and for the woman testosterone flows thru her, this would be the change.** If this happens, we will need to pay close attention to the consequences. Judges and public officials will then be required to recognize as a marriage any sexually Intimate bond between two people who want to call themselves married. Which means that there will no longer be any basis for distinguishing legally between a heterosexual union and a homosexual relationship, which means henceforth that there will be no legal basis for restrictions against a homosexual couple obtaining children in any way they choose for such restrictions would constitute discrimination?

# INTRODUCTION

And it will mean that when a mature mother and son, or father and daughter, or trio or quartet of partners comes to the courts or to the marriage-license bureau to ask that their sexually active relationship be recognized as marriage, there will be no legal grounds *of a non-arbitrary kind* to reject the requests. Because if it is now arbitrary and unjust to recognize heterosexual marriage as something exclusive and different from homosexual relationships, then it will be arbitrary and unjust not to grant the request of other partners to call their sexually intimate and enduring relationships marriage. But, of course, since legal declarations cannot turn reality into something it cannot become, a variety of conundrums, contradictions, and anomalies will inevitably arise. And the only way to resolve them will be to revise the law so it squares with, and does justice to, reality. And the reality is that the Kingdom of GOD principles are no longer a factor in the Sealed Indoctrinated Constitution of these United States of America and if the One who gave you "LIFE" is no longer a factor, if the One whom Heaven and Earth belongs to and everything in (He owns All) is no longer a factor, if this be the practice mind set of this people to ignore the Commandments of GOD with all your Heart (spirit), Mind (soul) and Body. **Then the question is: What do you think GODS response will be?** **The Parable of the Tenants: About the Kingdom of GOD** *[9]He went on to tell the people this parable: "A man planted a vineyard, rented it to some farmers and went away for a long time. [10] At harvest time he sent a servant to the tenants so they would give him some of the fruit of the vineyard. But the tenants beat him and sent him away empty-handed. [11] He sent another servant, but that one also they beat and treated shamefully and sent away empty-handed. [12] He sent still a third, and they wounded him and threw him out. [13] "Then the owner of the vineyard said, 'What shall I do? I will send my son, whom I love; perhaps they will respect him.'[14] "But when the tenants saw him, they talked the matter over.*

# INTRODUCTION

*'This is the heir,' they said. 'Let's kill him, and the inheritance will be ours.' [15] So they threw him out of the vineyard and killed him. "What then will the owner of the vineyard do to them? [16] He will come and kill those tenants and give the vineyard to others." When the people heard this, they said, "God forbid!" [17] Jesus looked directly at them and asked, "Then what is the meaning of that which is written:*

> *"The stone the builders rejected*
> *Has become the cornerstone*

*[18] Everyone who falls on that stone will be broken to pieces; anyone on whom it falls will be crushed."*
*[19] The teachers of the law and the chief priests looked for a way to arrest him immediately, because they knew he had spoken this parable against them. But they were afraid of the people. Luke 20:9-19*

# INTRODUCTION

"It may be said that the teaching of Jesus concerning the Kingdom of God represents his whole teaching. It is the main, determinative subject of all his discourse. His ethics were ethics of the Kingdom; his theology was theology of the Kingdom; his teaching regarding himself cannot be understood apart from his interpretation of the Kingdom of God" "This is our first basic thesis about Jesus: He did not preach about Himself, or simply about God, but about the Kingdom of God" According to the records of Jesus' ministry, the pioneer of the Christian faith, Jesus, gave a definite label to the Christian Gospel. He called it, quite specifically, "the Gospel (Good News) about the Kingdom of God." In Luke 16:16 Jesus remarked that since the time of John the Baptist (Matt. 3:2) "the Gospel of the Kingdom of God has been proclaimed." The Gospel of the Kingdom of God is another way of describing the hope of the Christian, and the plan of God upon earth. But you could easily miss this central and fundamental point, if you listened to contemporary versions of the Gospel. The vocabulary of modern proponents of Christianity and the Gospel avoids this basic vocabulary of Jesus. When is the last time you heard on radio, television or from the pulpit, the words "Gospel of (or about) the Kingdom"? Certainly the word Gospel is not in short supply. But the biblical description, in Matthew, Mark and Luke, of Jesus' saving Gospel — the Gospel about the Kingdom of God/Kingdom of Heaven — is almost extinct. Very few people know that the Kingdom of God and the Kingdom of Heaven are exactly equivalent, with no difference in meaning. Only Matthew uses the title Kingdom of Heaven, as the table below reveals. Below, in the left hand column, is every instance where the phrase "kingdom of heaven" occurs in the New Testament. As you can see, this phrase is unique to Matthew. Nowhere else in the Bible does the phrase "kingdom of heaven" occur. In the right hand column are those instances where parallel passages exist outside of Matthew. The term "Kingdom of Heaven" occurs 31 times in Matthew.

# INTRODUCTION

It is noteworthy that it appears nowhere else in the New Testament. In contrast, the term "Kingdom of God" occurs 63 times in the New Testament, 9 times in Acts and Paul's epistles, only 5 times in Matthew -- the balance being found in Mark, Luke and John. As to why Matthew preferred "kingdom of heaven" to "kingdom of God," the explanation has long been that Matthew, writing to specifically Jewish readers, inserted "heaven" for "God" so as not to offend the Jewish sensibilities regarding uttering the name of God or the term that describes Him. This is probably correct, but it leaves us with no explanation for the 5 times Matthew failed to make the switch, or for why he uses "God" in over 50 other instances. Nonetheless, as the above table makes it clear, if you compare the synoptic gospels -- Matthew, Mark and Luke, you will find that Matthew's "kingdom of heaven" exactly parallels Mark's and Luke's "kingdom of God." So there is no doubt that they are different terms describing the same thing.

The "kingdom of heaven" and "kingdom of God" are synonymous. Having established this truth, we still are left with the question, "What is the Kingdom of Heaven/God?" Before we answer this question, we should explain what the Kingdom of Heaven is not. The Kingdom of Heaven is not the same thing as heaven. When the New Testament uses the phrase "the Kingdom of Heaven" it is not referring to heaven. Instead it is referring to the Millennial Kingdom which has been ordained from heaven, that is, from God -- hence the interchangeability between "Kingdom of Heaven" and "Kingdom of God." Unfortunately too many people have heard a great deal of preaching and teaching about heaven as the hope of a Christian and consequently think that "the Kingdom of Heaven" and "heaven" are the same. They are not. The Kingdom of Heaven is a kingdom <u>from</u> heaven, not a kingdom <u>in</u> heaven. God reigns supreme in heaven. Heaven is the locus of His authority – the point from which He rules the universe. The words "of heaven" then are referring to the origin of this Kingdom.

# INTRODUCTION

It is the place from which the Kingdom is coming, not a destination to which we are going. So we see that although the Kingdom of Heaven is heavenly in character and origin, it is not the same thing as heaven. To avoid the confusion between heaven and the Kingdom of Heaven, and since the term "Kingdom of God" occurs much more frequently in the Bible, it is the "Kingdom of God" that is preferred when describing the future kingdom in which Jesus will reign as king. The "Kingdom of God" is the master-term in Jesus' presentation of the Christian faith. It is his constant slogan, the concept around which all of his discourse revolves. "Kingdom of God" is the phrase in which the genius of the faith is concentrated. Jesus bared his mind and the fundamental intention of his whole career as prophet, rabbi and Son of God with these precious words, which should be indelibly written on the hearts of his followers: "But He said to them, "I must preach the **kingdom of God** to the other cities also, for I was sent for this purpose." (Luke 4:43). Logically, then, the same driving purpose should be found within all Christian evangelism. Yet, strangely, the phrase "Gospel of the Kingdom of God" is absent from the lips of nearly all contemporary attempts to "preach salvation." This should tell us that something is seriously amiss in mainstream Christianity. If Jesus spoke of the Gospel of the Kingdom of God and made this the key for an intelligent reception of himself and his message, what is the Kingdom of God/Kingdom of Heaven? The Kingdom of God was a phrase well known to Jesus and his audience. The Kingdom of God was the national hope of Israel. It had been described in detail in the books of the Hebrew prophets (the Old Testament — actually "the Hebrew Bible"). Jesus did not play verbal games with his audience. He did not come into Galilee calling for repentance and belief in the Gospel about the Kingdom (Mark 1:14, 15) intending his audience to misunderstand his words! Common sense and honesty dictate that Jesus expected the audience to know what the Kingdom of God was.

# INTRODUCTION

Jesus did not define the Kingdom. There was no need to do this. The Kingdom of God meant "God's revolutionary Government" to be inaugurated by the promised Messiah on a renewed earth. (The Kingdom of God/Kingdom of Heaven certainly did not mean a realm of disembodied post-mortem spirits in Heaven.) The Kingdom of God was a future event, and a very spectacular one. It spelled destruction for the wicked and joy and endless life for the true followers of the Messiah: Luke 13:28 There shall be weeping and gnashing of teeth, when ye shall see Abraham, and Isaac, and Jacob, and all the prophets, in the **kingdom of God**, and you [yourselves] thrust out. The Kingdom of God involved Israel, the natural sons of Abraham:

> Acts 1:6 So when they met together, they asked him, "Lord, are you at this time going to restore **the kingdom to Israel**?"

The Kingdom of God was preached as residing upon this earth, not in heaven:

Luke 11:1-2 Our Father in heaven, hallowed be your name, your **kingdom** come, your will be done **on earth** as it is in heaven.

Revelation 5:9-10 By thy blood didst ransom men for God from every tribe and tongue and people and nation, and hast **made them a kingdom** and priests to our God, and **they shall reign on earth**.

The Kingdom of God was proclaimed as something that the righteous receive only <u>after</u> Jesus returns: Matthew 25:31-34 But **when the Son of Man comes in His glory**, and all the angels with Him, then He will sit on His glorious throne. And all the nations will be gathered before Him; and He will separate them from one another, as the shepherd separates the sheep from the goats; and He will put the sheep on His right, and the goats on the left.

# INTRODUCTION

Then the King will say to those on His right, 'Come, you who are blessed of My Father, inherit **the kingdom** prepared for you from the foundation of the world. The Kingdom of God was a key part of the Gospel.

It was what Jesus taught...

> Matthew 4:23 And Jesus went about all Galilee, teaching in their synagogues, and **preaching the gospel of the kingdom**,

...and it was what the apostles taught as an essential part of the Gospel...

> Acts 8:12 But when **they believed Philip preaching the things concerning the kingdom of God**, and the name of Jesus Christ, they were baptized, both men and women.

Acts 28:30-31 And **Paul** dwelt two whole years in his own hired house, and received all that came in unto him, **preaching the kingdom of God**, and teaching those things which concern the Lord Jesus Christ, with all confidence, no man forbidding him.

# PART I

# THE

# HETEROSEXUAL

# CHAPTER I
## THE PURPOSE FOR MAN

Until the restoration of earth and God's reconstitution of the heavenly lights, Lucifer, the "light-bearer" and his followers had found themselves in the dark, awaiting their fate. Satan's coup d'état had ended a dismal failure, and his nefarious experimentations on earth, the original Eden, had been summarily terminated by a divine intervention that left not only the earth but the surrounding universe as well buried in deep darkness. We know from the testimony of scripture that a trial followed in which God condemned Satan and his fallen angels for their rejection of His authority and for their rebellion:

> Behold, He does not place [unreserved] trust in His servants, but charges [even] His angels with error. Job 4:18

> Then He will say to those on His left, "Away from Me, you accursed ones, into the eternal fire [already] ***prepared for the devil and his angels***. Matthew 25:41

Concerning judgment, because the ruler of this world has been condemned. John 16:11  Satan's case (and that of his followers) has thus already been adjudicated and his ultimate fate pronounced. By the time he and his fallen angels are cast down to the earth during the Great Tribulation (Rev.12:7-9), he will be well aware of the fact that he has "but little time left" (Rev.12:12).

At the conclusion of human history, but not until that point has been reached at the end of the millennial rule of Christ, Satan will face the execution of his sentence (Rev.20:10; Is.24:21-22), a verdict adjudged before human history began. The question may well be posed, "why the delay in judgment? Why did God not simply plunge the devil and his minions into the fires of hell immediately after their just condemnation?" The answer to all such questions is intimately bound up with God's creation of another species of sentient, morally responsible creatures, namely, Man. So it is that to the purpose, creation and fall of mankind that we must now turn. Though already under sentence of death for his unrepentant attempt to overthrow God's rule over the universe (Job 4:18; Matt.25:41; Jn.16:11), Satan still retains his freedom of action. We find him spying on our first parents in the garden (Gen.3), appearing before the Lord to slander our brethren (Job 1&2; Zech.3; Rev.12:10), and prowling the earth in search of believers whose defenses are down (1Pet.5:8). The reason for the devil's intense interest in mankind is similar to the reason for our creation in the first place (and to the reason for the delay in carrying out the sentence of death under which he stands as well): *Man is meant as a response to Satan's rebellion*, a living refutation of the devil's slanderous lies against the character of God. God has created mankind 1) to demonstrate to all angelic kind His *ability to reconcile* His creatures to Himself, and 2) *to actually replace* all that was lost through the devil's defection. <u>Man created to demonstrate God's righteousness in acting mercifully</u>: Although every aspect of God's perfect character is visible in His gracious dealings with the human race, the demonstration of His righteousness toward us in salvation most directly answers Satan's slanders regarding God's ability to provide reconciliation. It will be remembered that part of the devil's appeal to his potential followers rested on his assurance that God would be unable to effect any reconciliation between Himself and His rebellious creatures.

Satan reasoned that God's righteousness would stand in the way of His mercy and thus make forgiveness impossible. God would thus be "put in a box", unable to act in mercy without compromise, unable to execute punishment without permanently marring His creation in an irreversible way. No matter how much He might dislike it, God would be forced to tolerate Satan's usurpation of power. And though it would not have formed part of his public pitch, the devil was no doubt also working on the "safety in numbers" principle, reckoning that while God might choose to chastise one rebel, removing the vast multitude of angels whom Satan had been able to recruit would create an irreparable rift in the fabric of the universe. But the devil's logic failed to take into account the ineffable love of God, and was oblivious to the idea that our God is a God of such grace that He would even sacrifice His most beloved possession, His Son, Jesus Christ, on our behalf. Satan was correct about the righteousness of God preventing His mercy from arbitrarily forgiving sin in any form, but what the devil did not count on was God's willingness to pay for sin Himself through the sacrifice of His Son, so that we might justly be accounted righteous in His eyes (2Cor.5:21):

> For I am not ashamed of the gospel, because it is the ***power*** whereby God may save everyone who believes (whether the Jew first, or the Greek). ***Because in it the righteousness of God is revealed*** from faith to faith, as it is written, "[it is he who is] righteous on account of his faith [who] shall live".
> Romans 1:16-17

We are saved by faith in the Person and work of the One who died in our place and paid the price of sin for us, our Lord and Savior Jesus Christ. Because Jesus paid the price, God can forgive our sin, not arbitrarily, but justly, since it has been paid for in full in the most precious coin.

God is therefore not only merciful to forgive us and welcome us into His family when we believe in Jesus, He is also just in justifying us, righteous in proclaiming us righteous, "not from works of righteousness which we have done" (Tit.3:5), but from our acceptance of the work of the One who died for us. Angels being angels, any decision to rebel against God would be final. Possessed as they are of perceptive abilities that far exceed our material limitations, it can be truly said of them that "they knew what they were getting into" (at least as far as creatures can know). Reconciliation of fallen angels to a merciful God was therefore never a likely possibility – because *they* would not have it, *not* because God could not or would not do it. The truth of this last point He has proven irrefutably by the loving sacrifice of His only Son on mankind's behalf, paying a price so steep we can only dimly comprehend it. If the devil and his angels had been of a mind to receive such an incomparable gesture of sacrifice and mercy, God would have generously provided it. By giving up His Son to the cross, God has demonstrated beyond any shadow of a doubt both His willingness and His ability to rescue His creatures, for He has in fact done so for us, even though it meant paying the price His righteousness demanded with the blood of His own Son. Thus human history is on the one hand a demonstration to angelic kind (elect as well as fallen) of God's mercy and His ability to act justly in providing that mercy (albeit at tremendous cost to Himself). We human beings are actually experiencing God's love and mercy as He provides for us here in the world despite the devil's opposition.

## The Purpose for Man

To the angels, however, we are a demonstration of that love and mercy, made effective through the sacrifice of Jesus Christ and our faith in Him. Being spirits and so not subject to the material limits that so try our human hearts of flesh, they must learn by observation, and observe us they do in great earnestness (Job 1&2; Matt.18:10; Lk.15:10; 1Cor.4:9; 11:10; 1Pet.1:12). That this demonstration will have been one of over seven thousand years' duration (when human history shall have finally run its course) is merely further proof of the graciousness and long-suffering of God (Is.30:18; Rom.2:4; 2Pet.3:9; 3:15 ). Through the long course of this demonstration (which is our collective human experience), the elect angels will have come to know God and His perfect character better than ever before, while the fallen angels will see their leader's every blasphemous accusation refuted and destroyed in voluminous detail. And when all is said and done, God's righteousness will have been affirmed as beyond reproach, proved beyond a shadow of a doubt in the merciful salvation of believing mankind. <u>Man created to replace Satan and his angels</u>: The creation of Man following the Genesis Gap judgment is a clear indication that the two events are intimately related. For God to create a new species of creature, possessing along with the angels both spirituality and free will, and then to deposit them on the very scene of Satan's rebellious activity was no subtle indication that at least one of God's purposes for mankind would be the replacement of the devil and his death demons. This must have been abundantly and immediately clear to Satan. For here was a new moral creature who (left to his own devices) might just do what he and his would not: *obey God's will without rebelling against Him*. As the requisite population was reached through procreation, Satan and company could be removed. Wholeness and completeness having thus been restored and Judgment, after all, had already been pronounced (Job 4:18; Matt.25:41; Jn.16:11).

What could remain except for a one-for-one replacement of fallen angels with human beings, once our numbers became sufficient? With judgment set, execution of God's sentence against the devil would be inevitable if not immediate (Rev.20:10): And it will come to pass on that day (i.e., the "day of the Lord"), that the Lord will punish the host of heaven above (i.e., the devil and his angels), and the kings of the earth below (i.e., those who have opposed His Christ), and they will be gathered together, bound in a dungeon, jailed and imprisoned. *And after many days they will be punished.* Isaiah 24:21-22 Therefore, with the creation of Man, a creature capable of procreation unlike the angels, the de facto removal of the only remaining, tangible barrier to Satan's execution was only a matter of time. The principle of God's desire to retrieve what is lost and replace what is missing is clearly seen in scripture in the parable of the lost sheep (Matt.18:12-14; Lk.15:4-10), the law of levirate marriage (Deut.25:5-6), and, of course, in His longing for all mankind to accept the gift of Jesus Christ and return to Him ( Ezek.18:23; Matt.18:14; Jn.12:47; 2Pet.3:9): [God] who wants all men to be saved and come to accept the truth. 1st Timothy 2:4 There is ample evidence to suggest that elect mankind is, in effect, replacing fallen angelic kind in God's universal order (Lk.10:17-20; 1Cor.6:3; Rev.20:4). The principle is most clearly seen in the God-Man's replacement of the original covering cherub: Lucifer (the "light bearer") replaced by the Morning Star, Jesus Christ (Is.14:12 with 2Pet.1:19; Rev.2:28; 22:16). Thus it is only fitting that the followers of the Morning Star should replace Lucifer's followers. In this way the wholeness and integrity of the creation will be restored, while everything that was lost will be replaced with something even better: willing worshipers of God in union with His Son, the God-Man, so that ultimately "God may be all in all" (1Cor.15:28).

*The Purpose for Man*

Satan's motives for precipitating the fall of Man are therefore clear. Unwilling to repent, neither could he afford to accept the new threat the status quo entailed. <u>Man created for the glory of God</u>: The replacement of Satan and his followers with willing worshipers, and the ample demonstration of God's love and righteousness through the sacrifice of His Son to save these sinful human beings abundantly redound to the great glory of God. After watching the events of human history unfold, the elect angels (and, in fact, all creatures) are moved to praise and glorify the Lord Almighty for His matchless grace (cf. Ps.148-150): To Him who sits on the throne and to the Lamb, be praise and honor and glory and power forever and ever! Revelation 5:13 NIV. It is for God's praise, for God's glory, that we have been created (<u>Is.60:21</u>; <u>Jn.17:10</u>; <u>21:19</u>; <u>Rom.9:23</u>). By making us and by saving us through Christ, God shows His love and exposes the devil's lies. In us, in what He has done for us, the glory of God shines forth, and those who love Him cannot help but praise Him:

> <u>Having foreordained us in [His] love for adoption to Himself through Jesus Christ according to the good pleasure of His will, for the purpose of producing **praise for the glory** of His grace which He has graciously bestowed on us in the Beloved [One]</u>. Ephesians 1:5-6

> <u>In whom we also have an inheritance, having been ordained according to the design of Him who is working everything out according to the desire of His will, that we who have previously placed our hope in Christ might serve the purpose of generating **praise for His glory**</u>. Ephesians 1:11-12

> <u>Everyone who is called by my Name, **for My glory I have created him**, I have formed him, indeed, I have made him</u>. Isaiah 43:7

*Save The Family*

As the passages above indicate, only *regenerate* human beings (i.e., believers in Christ) form the echelon of replacement for fallen angelic kind. Human beings who choose to reject God's gracious gift of Jesus Christ will share the fate of the devil and his followers in the lake of fire (Rev.20:11-15). This too is a part of the demonstration of the righteousness of God, and also redounds to His great glory. Not only will the entire universe witness His gracious provision of mercy towards all who turn to Him, but all who oppose His will, Satan and all rebels, be they angels or men, will be crushed materially (in judgment) as well as spiritually (through the demonstration of human history; Ps.76:10). And everyone, whether rebellious or regenerate, will eventually acknowledge the majesty, the righteousness, the glory of God:

> By Myself I have sworn. From my mouth a righteous word has gone forth, which will not be revoked, that every knee will bow to Me, and to Me every tongue will swear. And so they will acknowledge Me: "Only in the Lord are righteousness and might." Before Him will come all who raged against Him and they will be put to shame. Isaiah 45:23-24

It is in the nature of God not to let a lie stand, but instead to expose all lies to the blinding light of the truth. Human history constitutes, in effect, the "last judgment" of fallen angelic kind, a vivid, living demonstration of their error and utter sinfulness in the course of which "every mouth will be stopped" (every excuse destroyed: Rom.3:19; Ps.107:42; Mic.7:16) and at the end of which every knee will bow and tongue declare the glory of God and the grace of God in the gift of His Son our Lord Jesus Christ (Rom.14:11; Phil.2:10-11).

# CHAPTER II
# THE PURPOSE FOR THE WOMAN

God has a beautiful plan for womanhood that will bring order and fulfillment if it is followed in obedience. God's plan is that one man and one woman, of equal standing before Him but of different roles, should be bonded together as one. In His wisdom and grace He specifically created each for his or her role. At creation, God caused a deep sleep to fall on Adam, and from him God took a rib and made a woman (Genesis 2:2 1). She was a direct gift from the hand of God, made from man and for man (1 Corinthians 11:9). "Male and female created he them", (Genesis 1:27) each different but made to complete and complement each other. Although the woman is considered the "weaker vessel" (1 Peter 3:7), this does not make her inferior. She was made with a purpose in life that only she could fill. To woman has been given one of the greatest privileges in the world, that of molding and nurturing a living soul. Her influence, especially in the realm of motherhood, affects her children's eternal destination. Even though Eve brought condemnation upon the world with her act of disobedience, God considered women worthy of a part in the plan of redemption (Genesis 3:15). "But when the fullness of the time was come, God sent forth his Son, made of a woman." (Galatians 4:4). He entrusted to her the bearing of and the caring for his own dear Son. The woman's role is not insignificant! A distinction between the sexes is taught throughout the Bible. Paul teaches if a man has long hair, it is a shame unto him, but if a woman has long hair, it is a glory to her (1 Corinthians 11:14, 15). "The woman shall not wear that which pertained unto a man, neither shall a man put on a woman's garment: for all that do so are abominations unto the Lord thy God" (Deuteronomy 22:5). Their roles are not to be interchangeable. In the Garden of Eden, God said, "It is not good that the man should be alone," and He made a help meet for him-a companion, someone to satisfy his needs

(Genesis 2:18). Proverbs 31:10-31 tells in detail what kind of help meet the woman is to be. The supportive role of the wife to the husband is very evident in this description of the ideal woman. She "will do him good and not evil." Because of her honesty, modesty and chastity, "her husband doth safely trust in her." By her efficiency and diligence she would look well to her household. The basis for her virtue is found in verse 30: "a woman that feared the Lord." This is a reverential fear that gives meaning and purpose to her life. Only as the Lord lives in her heart can she be the woman she was meant to be. To become a child of God she needs to repent, confess her sins and accept Christ through faith. With Christ she will be able to live a self-denied life. The Holy Spirit will give strength, courage, and direction to fulfill her duties. He will grace her life with humility, modesty, and with that inner "ornament of a meek and quiet spirit, which is in the sight of God of great price" (1 Peter 3:3, 4). Proper, modest dress adds to the hidden charm of a woman. She should never draw attention to her body by being overdressed or underdressed. To avoid confusion and establish order, someone needs to be the head and God has ordained that this should be the man (1 Corinthians 11:3). Marriage is to be a harmonious relationship similar to that of Christ and the Church. Christ is subject to God, man is subject to Christ, and woman is subject to man. Why would any woman rebel at her position in the framework of authority when even Christ, the Son, is subject to the Father? As the wife reverences her husband, she is obedient to the scripture (Ephesians 5:33), and her husband is then able to bear the responsibility that God has laid on his shoulders. The liberation movement has challenged God's blueprint for womanhood. Women are clamoring for freedom and fulfillment by asking for total equality. This puts them into a power struggle- into a competitive role instead of a complementary partnership. Their quest for freedom only leads them into bondage.

## The Purpose for the Woman

Nevertheless, the selfishness and ungodliness of many men is without excuse. In this context some of women's frustrations can be understood. Ironically, the very thing that many women are rejecting is God's way of establishing the woman in a life that fully satisfies. If a women moves aggressively into the man's world and there seeks independence and equality, she loses her femininity that reserved, modest sweetness that men respect and God approves. Fulfillment comes as she cultivates those gifts for which she was created. A woman's submission to her husband liberates her from a multitude of frustrating problems, and her submission to God's order frees her from guilt. Submission is a blessing, not a curse! The pattern of men taking the leadership and women following will bring a blessing to single women as well as married women, to daughters as well as wives. As an outward sign of this submission and her submission to Christ, the Christian woman is commanded to have her head covered for praying and prophesying (1 Corinthians 11:3-5). Man is subject to Christ and should therefore pray with his head uncovered. Woman is subject to man and should pray with her head covered. Wearing a head covering is recognition of this divine order. Love in marriage is to be pure and is given for pleasure as well as for propagation. Woman was uniquely created for the special task of bearing children, a creative fulfillment. God said, "Be fruitful and multiply" (Genesis 1:28). To purposely choose not to have children is sidestepping God's principle and forfeiting one of the most rewarding experiences in a woman's life. Woman's first duty is the making and keeping of her home. Many a modern woman chooses a career, hires a baby-sitter, and rushes her children through childhood so that she can be free to pursue her selfish interests. The Bible teaches that women are to be "keepers at home" (Titus 2:5). This means a women is to be there, loving her husband, teaching and enjoying her children, and applying the homemaking arts with joy in her heart. This mother is the heartbeat of the home. She helps lay the foundation of moral standards there.

*Save The Family*

The warmth of her spirit quietly establishes security in the lives of little children-confidence, that in spite of their problems and fears, all will be right. Why would any woman trade this noble place for some dollars earned or for some coveted position? This Bible way is not just being old-fashioned; it is God's order. The women who wholeheartedly accept God's plan will be blessed. In certain instances, a woman's role extends beyond her home. Examples are given in both the Old and New Testaments of godly women who had responsibilities in God's kingdom. Also today there is a place for the Christian woman to serve within the Church. As she exercises her inborn attributes of love, gentleness, and compassion, she is a living example of that which becomes godliness. Older women are exhorted to teach the young women, "that the word of God be not blasphemed" (Titus 2:4,5). Single Christian women, who do not have the cares of a home and a family, are able to fill a special place (1 Corinthians 7:34). There are definite guidelines for women's behavior in the Church. They are not to usurp authority over men. Paul instructs, "Let your women keep silence in the churches" (1 Corinthians 14:34,35; 1 Timothy 2:11-15). The order that God has planned for women excludes them from preaching. Faithful women find places for active participation in Christian service where they can humbly and consistently fellowship with other Christians. May each woman fill her role with the grace of God in her heart, live in submissive obedience to His will, and humbly give of herself in the daily practices of life. As each person fills his respective place in God's plan, there is beautiful harmony that emerges in the heart, the home, and the church.

*The Purpose for the Woman*

**THE WOMAN.,** When the wounded family comes in, the position of the woman steps in with her nurturing ways and means, the woman releases the love, the care, the compassion for the need of the family doing this time of difficulty, she express peace and joy to the kids who so yearn for her attention 24hrs a day. She carries the burden of comfort to every corner of the home that where ever Devil seeks to enter he will know that there is a battle ready suitable helper, woman and wife in that place with a love for her family and that she will not be compromised. The woman is the engineer of the home, as the Bibles says— in Prov. 14:1, "The wise woman builds her house, but with her own hands the foolish one tears hers down," But Prov. 9:1-6 says— " Wisdom has built her house; she has set up its seven pillars. She has prepared her meat and mixed her wine; she has also set her table. She has sent out her servants, and she calls from the highest point of the city, "Let all who are simple come to my house!" To those who have no sense she says," come; eat my food and drink of the wine I have mixed. Forsake your folly and live, and proceed in the way of understanding." The woman given the proper supplies from her husband sets the standards as to how the house runs or operates amongst the children, the husband sets the instructions out to the suitable helper which in intern dissect the instruction to the simplest form to the woman who then gathers all information transitioning it in her thinking, to her attitude, to her philosophy, to behavior and her action. This gives the woman what she needs to build her house in to a home, fulfilling all needs to the every aspect of the **"Husband and Child"** so that her virtuous ways and means can exceed to the ways of the Old as Paul says. In— **1 Pet 3:1-6; GODLY LIVING in the same way, you wives, be submissive to your own husbands so that even if any of them are disobedient to the word, they may be won without a word by the behavior of their wives, as they observe your chaste and respectful behavior.**

*Save The Family*

**Your adornment must not be merely external-braiding the hair, and wearing gold jewelry, or putting on dresses; but let it be the hidden person of the heart, with the imperishable quality of a gentle and quiet spirit, which is precious in the sight of God. For in this way in former times the holy woman also, who hoped in God, used to adorn themselves, being submissive to their own husbands; just as Sarah obeyed Abraham, calling him lord, and you have become her children if you do what is right without being frightened by any fear.** What 1 Peter 3 is saying here is that this is the intended way of life for the woman to operate in; it is this mannerism that is acceptable with God and pleasing in his sight. Such differences or division hinders the prayers that the family seeks God to interfere in the families affairs; the woman is the heart of this threefold position of the female (suitable helper, woman and wife). But it is vitally important for the woman in her position to operate to the fullest, it is important to understand the husband's instructions for such instructions come from God as the husband is in line with the kingdom of God. The woman in her early rise is for the sake of instructions for the days family business, everything about the woman in her position is to transcend the family as to God the Father, in the name of Christ Jesus under the instructions of the Holy Spirit which is the instructions to the husbands which is instructions to the suitable helper, woman and wife to maintain the family. The greatest downfall of the family is division; division is to set apart; to separate, this is what we witness in the Garden of Eden with Adam and Eve. This division was so catastrophic to the human race, not God's purpose and plan but to man, leaving Adam and Eve under a great punishment that still stands today Gen. 3:1-23; (this is not a part of the curse) which redirected God original intention for the foundation of the family, altering temporarily, how the family should function. This fall occurred by way of the two standing together as one to eat of the fruit that made them like the trinity, as God said knowing good and evil.

## The Purpose for the Woman

This fall came by way of the suitable helper not the woman or the wife, "The wise woman builds her house, but with her own hands the foolish one tears hers down" (Prov. 14:1). Some of the world finest couples are divorced more than once and their families have been sacrificed for their job. This is hard enough for a man, but a woman has the authority of her husband and the authority she serves at work. Some would say that they have no problem in this area, but the rise in broken homes says much different. God intended the home to be the center of a women's world. This has been greatly attacked even in the days of the New Testament. In Titus 5:14 younger women were encouraged to marry, bear children, and guide the home so that they would not be attacked by the enemy. In Titus 2:5, older women were to encourage the younger women to love their husband and children and to be keepers of the home that the word of God might not be blasphemed. Why? Because they were not doing what Paul was trying to do, lead them back to God's design. It is when we as a society have rejected His plan that our plan will be in the opposite direction and will lead to disaster. One of these ways is when we justify women working outside of the home. 40 years ago most young women were graduating from high school, getting married and starting to raise a family. Today, however, our society is teaching them that they need a career to fall back on just in case their marriage does not last. What does the word of God say will happen when women work outside the home? **The woman does not meet her highest potential,** God designed the woman to be a helpmeet for her husband. Often you hear women say that they are tired of being identified as somebody's wife, and they have forgotten that they will be the only one in the world that will hold that title in the family? If a husband were to lose their job, the company would just hire another person to replace him and within a short time he would be forgotten.

## Save The Family

If the family loses the husband, they would be damaged and would never be their best in moving forward. The absence would be felt for years to come. **The women of the house would then form an independent spirit**, the scriptures tell us that for Husband to love your wives. . . . Wives submit to your husband (Col. 3:18-19). Not even men are to be independent. Nowhere in scripture does God want an independent person, but our adversary, the devil, promotes independence from God. This is a damaging philosophy in marriages today. When a woman does not think she needs her husband or children, she will lose her love for them. This is one of the reasons why a growing number of couples do not have children. It reduces their independence and increases their so called freedom. **She becomes financially unwise;** This leads to a wakeup call to men that they should not to leave their wives, because of the hardships that they will bring upon them. Remember, she is your companion (best friend) and the wife of your covenant (Mal. 2:14). Many people lose sight on understanding how family should survive any level income, and or learn how to actually do better than most with two incomes. **The women of the house would then form an independent spirit**, the scriptures tell us that for Husband to love your wives. . . . Wives submit to your husband (Col. 3:18-19). Not even men are to be independent. Nowhere in scripture does God want an independent person, but our adversary, the devil, promotes independence from God. This is a damaging philosophy in marriages today. When a woman does not think she needs her husband or children, she will lose her love for them. This is one of the reasons why a growing number of couples do not have children. It reduces their independence and increases their so called freedom. **She becomes financially unwise;** This leads to a wakeup call to men that they should not to leave their wives, because of the hardships that they will bring upon them. Remember, she is your companion (best friend) and the wife of your covenant (Mal. 2:14).

## The Purpose for the Woman

Many people lose sight on understanding how family should survive any level income, and or learn how to actually do better than most with two incomes. **The Women's greatest asset is hindered**, with time is our most valuable asset and the Bible tells us to number our days that we may apply our hearts to wisdom (Psalms 90:12). God has placed in every women the gifts and talents to teach and train her children, not the daycare system. Scripture teaches that when a child is left to himself, he will bring his mother to shame (Proverbs 29:15). The Hebrew word for left is translated Shalach which means to send away. When women send their children out from their God given responsibilities it will bring shame to her. Women cannot fulfill their responsibility unless their husbands establish a platform for them to do that. We, as a nation, have forgotten the influencing power women have over her children and what mighty things she can accomplish for her community and the Kingdom of God when she has a platform in the home. **Women can be tempted to transfer her affections away from their husbands.** This is something that happens all over our nation: women having affairs with men in the work place. This is a major cause that lead up to an affair. As people work together, they talk and become friends. As problems develop at home, usually financial, discussions take place and soon she starts comparing the men at work to her husband. Even though an affair may never take place, she has misplaced some of her affections away from her husband and has damaged her marriage. Soon the husband realizes that she doesn't depend on him like she used to. Distrust and even jealousy raises its ugly head. When women get together and talk about their husband's it's usually in a negative outcome. They disgrace themselves, because they are degrading the one that they vowed to love, cherish and honor for the rest of their lives before GOD. **This brings on an automatic punishment by way of adultery from the hand of GOD.**

## Save The Family

When Adam and Eve sinned, God cursed man that he would work by the sweat of his brow and the woman would have pain in child bearing. Now the working woman has taken both of the curses upon herself. God's word never said that women could not perform an outside job or that they weren't as smart as men. In fact, God has put women in roles that were designed for men when they would not lead. This book is for men and women who are committed to Jesus Christ and are seeking to make a difference in their lives for Him. Jesus said seek first the Kingdom of heaven and his righteousness and all these things shall be added to you Matt. 6:33. We as Christians need to stop following after the things of the world and start to deny ourselves pick up the Cross and follow Christ. If you find this offensive, then this message is not for you. When we began to put our lives under Biblical principles, only then can God step in and bless you and your family. Simply because of you showing honor and glory to which He is, GOD Almighty. We can truly be the light of the world that He wants us to be. When children see that parents are committed to each other and they can come home to a mother who is there to make them the best that they can be, then they will rise up and call her blessed. To the separated or divorced women, this message is for your husband's to return to their vows and allow God to be the God of love that He longs to be. To the widow, this message is for family, friends and the Church to return to their Citizen of the Kingdom of GOD duties and support these women.

# CHAPTER III

## The Purpose for Sex

**God** created us with the desire for sex, and we ought to understand his design that was meant for us in our relationships with others about sex. Christians absolutely need to seek God's purpose in this area of their lives. God created us male and female and because of that we will be attracted to one another, why? We are the opposite sex and it is a part of creation that woman was made for man as a part of creation. But we must learn to control our desires because having sex, and even the desire for sex with someone outside of marriage is not God's plan. God created man in his own image; in the image of God he created him; male and female he created them. God blessed them and said to them: **Be Fruitful and Multiply, and Replenish the Earth** (Genesis 1:26-30). God intends for a married man and woman to have sexual relations for the purpose of replenishing the earth within the confines of marriage. God wants us to have sex so we will bring forth more children into the world for him and to teach and train our children up in the wisdom of God! Had Adam and Eve decided to not have sex and have children then essentially they would have been rebelling against God's purpose and instruction. **Controlling our Sex Drive**, even though sex is good, it must be controlled! As we look at society we see many uncontrolled desires and sex drives running amok causing much harm and danger. People blame God for plagues and diseases but these things are caused from your own rebelliousness toward GOD! When we choose to disobey God's commands things happens because of our own foolish choices, as the bible tells us "There are ways that seems right to a man but in the end, it leads to death. Prov. 14:12. Sex outside of marriage may seem so right to one but it is against the Law of GOD, you break the law you automatically start the process of punishment brought on by the hand of GOD.

*Save The Family*

As with anything in life we must control it, so it will not overtake our lives and cause spiritual and emotional turmoil for us. We must control our sex drive, lest we hurt others, damage our relationships and ourselves, and sin against God. If we don't control our appetite for food we become overweight and sick. In the same way if we don't control our appetite for sex it will control us and tempt us into immoral acts of lust. That lust will lead to other things that many are not prepared to handle. More dangerous if this thing lead to danger for all parties involved. Did you know that your bodies are members of Christ himself? Shall I then take the members of Christ and unite them with a prostitute? Never! Do you know that he who unites himself with a prostitute is one with her in body? For it is said, "The two will becomes one flesh." But he who unites himself with lord is one with him in spirit. Paul uses this incident with the Corinthian church immorality ways and means to bring out GODs certification in marriage. GOD certifies a union by way of sexual relations between a man and a woman. It is the law of the land that certifies a marriage by way of documentation such as a marriage license. Does GOD recognize the law of the land? Absolutely, Paul speaks of in the book of it in Rom. 13:1, "Everyone must submit himself to the governing authorities, for there is no authority except that which God has established. The authorities that exist have been established by GOD." God says that sex is a beautiful and healthy part of life when it is between a married man and woman. But he also lets us know that **the sex drive must be used for his purpose Fornication** is sexual intercourse between two unmarried people "the defrauding of each other". Many of us think about things with a different perspective than what many have been brought up to believe, sex without any real intention for marriage is a deception and is morally wrong. This is why God calls fornication a sin. Sex outside of the boundaries of marriage will lead the hand of GOD against you. God does not want to see us heart broken or sick from disease because we gave into sexual immorality.

## The Purpose for Sex

God loves us and wants what is best for us, to reserve having sex until we are married. "For this is the will of God, that you should be sanctified: that you should avoid sexual immorality; that each of you should learn to control his own body in a way that is holy and honorable, not in passionate lust like the heathen, who do not know GOD; and that in this matter no one should wrong his brother or take advantage of him. The Lord will punish men for all such sins, as we have already told you and warned you. For GOD did not call us to be impure, but to live a holy life. (1 Thessalonians 4:3-7). Marriage is the only intended purpose for sex. Anything else perverts and distorts sexual relations and the mind, body and spirit of a person. God created sex for sexual enjoyment in marriage. The bottom line is our sex drive was created for the purpose of procreation and sexual fulfillment between a husband and a wife! Realizing the proper use of our sex drive is the first step in controlling it. Then the Lord GOD made a woman from the rib he had taken out of the man, and he brought her to the man. Then man said, "This is now bone of my bones and flesh of my flesh; she shall be called woman, for she was taken out of man." For this reason a man will leave his father and mother and be united to his wife, and they will become one flesh. The man and his wife were both naked, and they felt no shame. (Genesis 2:23-25). The sex drive is not dirty, until we choose to abuse it. The sex drive is not sinful, until we choose to abuse it. Our sex drive is an awesome gift from God that should be used to honor and glorify God with by bringing forth children, and for our own enjoyment in marriage. **The institution of marriage** allows the lawful sexual union between male and female in the eyes of God and society. Since both, male and female should dedicate their lives to the Will of God and the great struggle in the journey of the meeting with God, the great struggle of the union between the two, then the pleasure derived from sex is Divinely given to enhance the union as well as to re-charge the electrical energy of the male and the female that they might continue the great journey and struggle of life.

These two, properly motivated, allows the sexual union to be a life-giving experience not only in procreation and continuance of the life of the species, but, it is invigorating as well as life giving to the marriage and the struggle of these two to become as one. To look at marriage as only the legalization of the sex act is to put our minds on a level that will not bring the best out of the experience. To become extreme in our view that the sex act is only for procreation and not meant by God to give pleasure to married couples is a view that is not in accord with the Will, Plan and Purpose of God. These pleasure centers in the human being, used properly and in accord with the Will of God, brings comfort, ease, consolation, rest, reward and joy to the souls that are working hard to fulfill their Divine duty and obligation. **What is the purpose of sex in marriage? 1.** Procreation of human species. **2.** Reward the struggle of the two to become one with the joy of the pleasure of each other's complimentary nature. **3.** To give rest, relaxation and new energy to the male to continue the great mission of being producer of mastering the earth and its laws as we strives to become one who stands in the place of God at his level of development. The female in energizing the male and giving him this comfort, consolation; giving him peace and quiet of mind as a rest period between struggle is also satisfied and is pleased because she has given rest to him to work for God, her and the family. Therefore, she is rested in herself. This is the Divine Purpose of Sex in Marriage. Satan, however, has taken this natural gift of God and made mischief with it causing us to go after pleasure without struggle; without the burden or responsibility of being what God created us to be. We have become pleasure seekers without responsibility and misusing our pleasure centers thus becoming slaves of pleasure. This has given rise to the misuse of women and the misuse of what God gave them for the man so that she becomes a prostitute – sex for hire, he becomes a pimp – using her and the need of the male for pleasure as a means of livelihood.

## The Purpose for Sex

The lust for pleasure is causing the abuse of children, male and female, and the misuse of our bodies. As a result, we are living in a morally degenerate world. We are paying the price for this moral degeneracy through the plague of AIDS and sexually transmitted diseases, which produce the destruction of the male and female and the destruction of our future. This is why we must return to God and seek to know His purpose for what He created and use everything of creation in accord with His purpose for it. Then, and only then, will we find the genuine peace, joy, and happiness that we seek. Psalms says, **"Behold, how good and how pleasant it is for brethren to dwell together in unity!"** Unity awards us another kind of pleasure. There is tremendous pleasure in being one with God. There is tremendous joy in knowing that we are pleasing in His sight. Let us strive for the real pleasure of life that comes from duty to God through his Son Christ Jesus; duty to ourselves; duty to our mates; duty to our families; duty to our community. Let us seek real pleasure that comes when we know that we have struggled to obey God; we have struggled to bear the burden of the great responsibility that God has placed on our shoulders; we have accepted the difficulty factor of life knowing truly that after difficulty comes ease. What is marriage for? The answer that you'll get from children's stories is, "to live happily ever after." The answer we get from television and movies is, "to make your life miserable ever after." No two people get married in order to make themselves or each other miserable. They marry with optimism that life truly will be more meaningful and emotionally richer. Before the 1960"s, the divorce rate was a lot lower than it is today and most couples reported being fairly happy together. But then the Sexual Revolution came along and people said, "We don't need marriage anymore. Anyone can live together for however long they want to for whatever reason they want to and shouldn't have to be bound together 'till death do us part."

*Save The Family*

We want freedom to express ourselves anyway we choose. We don't need God or the institution of marriage that He created." Then the minority of people who were unhappily married or who grew up in an unhappy home led the rebellion. They took over the legislatures; they took over the judicial system, they took over the entertainment industry and popular culture. They took over the schools, they have told us lie after lie in order to try to convince us that their own immoral behaviors are OK. Since this war on marriage and family began they dragged our culture down deeper and deeper into the gutter. Even though the average American's lifestyle is not like TV shows and movies make it out to be Hollywood continues to portray us that way. They are constantly pushing their immorality on us. The message is clear: If you aren't sexually promiscuous then shame on you. In addition, Hollywood exports this false view of Americans to the rest of the world. One of the major reasons there so many enemies in the Christian, Muslim, Judaism and Asian cultures is that they think we are all a bunch of sex addicts and perverts. They don't realize that most Americans are not like that. I believe one of the gravest mistakes occurred when we lost sight of God's purposes for marriage and sex. As a result, many people see marriage and sex inside of marriage as too limiting. They say things like, "God is against sex" and "God doesn't want us to have any fun." They don't think that their needs can be met through marriage. They use various alternatives to try to meet those needs on their own. But when we gain a correct view of God's purposes for marriage, only then can we realize how God uses marriage to protect us and provide for us better than any way we can devise on our own. God tells us why He created the institution of marriage. God has at least 5 purposes for marriage and sex that are found in Genesis chapters one and two.

*The Purpose for Sex*

**The Trinity** being first purpose for marriage and sex is to reflect God's oneness. Genesis tells us, "Then God said, 'Let us make man in our image, in our likeness.' " In order to understand oneness that two people can experience in a relationship together we need to understand God who makes that possible. To do that, we'll have to dive right in to some pretty heavy theology. You've learned somewhere that God has three persons yet is one God. Does this mean Christians can't count? Does this mean we believe in three Gods or one God? The doctrine of God's trinity can be very confusing but once we begin to understand it we see how God experiences the ultimate oneness in relationship. In order to make any sense of this, we have to distinguish between what the one refers to and what the three refers to. The one refers to God's essence or nature, in other words, His Goodness, His divine essence. No one else in the spiritual or physical universe has the divine essence. Indeed, there cannot be any other because there is no room for any more beings with a divine essence. God's divine essence takes up the whole universe. The divine essence cannot be divided between more than one god; otherwise it is not truly the divine essence. It is not that God is merely characterized by a divine essence; God is the divine essence and the divine essence is God. The three refers to three distinct persons. All the persons of the triune God share the divine essence. There is only one divine essence, but there are three persons who share this same nature. The members of the trinity are distinct (The Father, the Son and the Holy Spirit). Does it sound like I just contradicted myself? I haven't because the difference is this. The gods of mythology are distinct beings that act independently. They each have their own agenda. They are seen scheming against and fighting with each other. In 180 degree contrast, the members of the trinity are perfectly and deeply interrelated.

They have an unbreakable unity it is said, "For in the divine life there is no isolation, no insulation, no secretiveness, and no fear of being transparent to another." So while each of the divine persons (Father, Son, and Holy Spirit) fully similarly...We cannot remove one person from this intimate relationship and have the other two remain intact....Because the members of the Trinity share the same essence and mutually indwell one another, they also act as one rather than in isolation from one another. Even though three distinct wills exist within the Trinity, only one will is ultimately expressed, which indicates the deep unity of the Godhead. So we could answer the question: What is God like? By saying, "a triangle," but a triangle isn't personal. Instead, God answers the question with, "I am giving you a marriage relationship not just to know intellectually what I am like but to experience what I am like." What a teacher! In a marriage relationship we can experience the wonder and beauty of being two distinct individuals with two distinct wills being united by sharing the essence of humanness. God wants the marriage relationship to be the earthly, visible, tangible model for this ultimate oneness. God made mankind in such a way that males and females are distinctly different. So when a man and a woman come together they are two distinctly different people with not only personality differences but gender differences as well. When these two distinctly different genders are brought together they begin to reflect God's oneness. Genesis 1:26 - 28 tells us, "Then God said, 'Let us (the triune God) make man in our image, in our likeness...' So God created man in his own image, in the image of God he created him; male and female he created them."An individual, while made in the     image of God, can not reflect God's oneness. **A man and a man or a woman and a woman can not reflect God's oneness. Homosexuality can not reflect God's oneness. Instead, it is a counterfeit because to reflect God's oneness requires a male and a female. Why settle for less than the real thing?**

*The Purpose for Sex*

Now how does this oneness in relationship protect and provide for us? We are emotional and social creatures. We are made to love and to be loved. We are made for oneness with another person. But this oneness can't happen in one night. It takes a commitment to be loyal and faithful to only one person. This commitment is called marriage. This oneness doesn't even happen completely on a honeymoon. It takes years of getting to know each other, working together, living together, fighting together, relating together to experience the true depth of that deep oneness that is possible. So through marriage our needs for deep intimacy and emotional connectedness are met better than any other way. I'd better say something brief about celibacy here so I'm not misunderstood Celibacy is a God-given exception. It is a calling and a choice. Because God calls a person to celibacy He will take care of that person's needs for deep intimacy and emotional connectedness through His relationship with that person. Moving on, tragically, many young people mistakenly assume that just because their parents don't share emotional intimacy then no one, including them, can find it in marriage. It doesn't have to be that way. My fiancée' and I have had our ups and downs but through it all we have come to experience a deep emotional intimacy beyond what we ever thought was possible as we move toward being married. To achieve oneness on our own without God whether inside or outside of marriage, we rob ourselves of what we are made for. God designed marriage to protect us and provide for us.

**In Genesis** we read, "God blessed them and said to them, Be fruitful and increase in number; fill the earth." The second purpose for marriage and sex is to procreate, that is to make babies and thereby keep mankind from becoming extinct. The first purpose is to be productive in the world, plant some seeds that they grow to make an impact in the world. Over the years, a married couple has sex far more often than for the purpose of producing children.

If sex was only for procreation, God had to make it enjoyable so that we would want to do it more often than just for children. Procreation multiplies a godly heritage. Part of God's strategic plan is that through this lineage of godly descendants, Satan's evil rebellion would be defeated. You see, according to various passages in the Bible we learn that before the physical universe was created, God created the angels, including Lucifer, whose name meant "bearer of light," "Morning Star" He was the most awesome angel there was. He got conceited and led a third of all the angels in a coup attempt to replace God as the ultimate ruler of the universe. If he had really understood God he wouldn't have tried such a foolish and futile act. Instead of locking them up in prison or wiping them out of their very existence, God formulated a plan. Remember, Lucifer, who is now called Satan, meaning the adversary or opponent, isn't like God. He doesn't know the future and can't figure out God's plan. He may not know anymore about God's plan than we know, and that's reassuring. Anyway, part of God's strategy for dealing with this rebellion was to create the physical universe and planet earth and particularly mankind. God simply hasn't given us enough information to completely understand how this is important to His strategy but He isn't obligated to inform us or Satan of His battle plans. One thing is for sure, Satan hates God and anything that reminds him of God. It just so happened that God created mankind in his image, that is, to be finite replicas of the infinite God. So every time a new human being is conceived in its mother's womb there is another replica of God. So God told us to fill the earth with images of Himself. Can you imagine anything else that would drive Satan crazier than to turn every corner and see a reminder of the very God he hates? God made humans to be uniquely different than all other living things. Angels cannot reproduce and make more angels. And while sexual reproduction is important to all living creatures it is given a cosmic significance when it comes to human reproduction.

## The Purpose for Sex

When humans have sex to make babies it takes on the most mysterious meaning of making other humans that bear God's image. This is why abortion is wrong. It treats a human baby like the flesh of any other animal when instead it is a person that bears God's image. It delights Satan when babies are killed because then he doesn't have to risk the possibly of them growing up to become Christians and joining the fight against him. There is yet another reason God gave us sex and that is, to teach us to give unselfishly to one another. God endowed men and women with certain anatomical parts that produce pleasure but are not necessary for intercourse and procreation. Humans have the ability to prolong sex and to give and receive mutual pleasure. We can express love and affection by giving pleasure to our mate that goes way beyond what is necessary to simply make babies. Both marriage partners enjoy sex more when they learn to give and receive this extra pleasure. Their relationship is enriched and deepened as they learn to give to each other. Now how does this oneness in relationship protect and provide for us? We are emotional and social creatures. We are made to love and to be loved. We are made for oneness with another person. But this oneness can't happen in one night. It takes a commitment to be loyal and faithful to only one person. This commitment is called marriage. This oneness doesn't even happen completely on a honeymoon. It takes years of getting to know each other, working together, living together, fighting together, relating together to experience the true depth of that deep oneness that is possible. So through marriage our needs for deep intimacy and emotional connectedness are met better than any other way. I'd better say something brief about celibacy here so I'm not misunderstood. Celibacy is a God-given exception. It is a calling and a choice. Because God calls a person to celibacy He will take care of that person's needs for deep intimacy and emotional connectedness through His relationship with that person.

Moving on, tragically, many young people mistakenly assume that just because their parents don't share emotional intimacy then no one, including them, can find it in marriage. It doesn't have to be that way. My fiancée' and I have had our ups and downs but through it all we have come to experience a deep emotional intimacy beyond what we ever thought was possible as we move toward being married. To achieve oneness on our own without God whether inside or outside of marriage, we rob ourselves of what we are made for. God designed marriage to protect us and provide for us.

**In Genesis** we read, "God blessed them and said to them, Be fruitful and increase in number; fill the earth." The second purpose for marriage and sex is to procreate, that is to make babies and thereby keep mankind from becoming extinct. The first purpose is to be productive in the world, plant some seeds that they grow to make an impact in the world. Over the years, a married couple has sex far more often than for the purpose of producing children. If sex was only for procreation, God had to make it enjoyable so that we would want to do it more often than just for children. Procreation multiplies a godly heritage. Part of God's strategic plan is that through this lineage of godly descendants, Satan's evil rebellion would be defeated.

You see, according to various passages in the Bible we learn that before the physical universe was created, God created the angels, including Lucifer, whose name meant "bearer of light," "Morning Star" He was the most awesome angel there was. He got conceited and led a third of all the angels in a coup attempt to replace God as the ultimate ruler of the universe. If he had really understood God he wouldn't have tried such a foolish and futile act. Instead of locking them up in prison or wiping them out of their very existence, God formulated a plan.

## The Purpose for Sex

Remember, Lucifer, who is now called Satan, meaning the adversary or opponent, isn't like God. He doesn't know the future and can't figure out God's plan. He may not know anymore about God's plan than we know, and that's reassuring. Anyway, part of God's strategy for dealing with this rebellion was to create the physical universe and planet earth and particularly mankind. God simply hasn't given us enough information to completely understand how this is important to His strategy but He isn't obligated to inform us or Satan of His battle plans. One thing is for sure, Satan hates God and anything that reminds him of God. It just so happened that God created mankind in his image, that is, to be finite replicas of the infinite God. So every time a new human being is conceived in its mother's womb there is another replica of God. So God told us to fill the earth with images of Himself. Can you imagine anything else that would drive Satan crazier than to turn every corner and see a reminder of the very God he hates? God made humans to be uniquely different than all other living things. Angels cannot reproduce and make more angels. And while sexual reproduction is important to all living creatures it is given a cosmic significance when it comes to human reproduction. When humans have sex to make babies it takes on the most mysterious meaning of making other humans that bear God's image. This is why abortion is wrong. It treats a human baby like the flesh of any other animal when instead it is a person that bears God's image. It delights Satan when babies are killed because then he doesn't have to risk the possibly of them growing up to become Christians and joining the fight against him. There is yet another reason God gave us sex and that is, to teach us to give unselfishly to one another. God endowed men and women with certain anatomical parts that produce pleasure but are not necessary for intercourse and procreation. Humans have the ability to prolong sex and to give and receive mutual pleasure.

*Save The Family*

We can express love and affection by giving pleasure to our mate that goes way beyond what is necessary to simply make babies. Both marriage partners enjoy sex more when they learn to give and receive this extra pleasure. Their relationship is enriched and deepened as they learn to give to each other. Genesis 1:26 tells us, God blessed them and said to them, "Be fruitful and increase in number; fill the earth and subdue it. Rule over the fish of the sea and the birds of the air and over every living creature that moves on the ground." Lions are not the king of the beasts, humans are. Even though God built many self-managing checks and balances into nature He put mankind in charge of nature. Instead of managing His creation Himself, God chose to delegate the task to mankind. What a responsibility! In chapter 2 of Genesis we learn that man was created to be a steward of the land. Even before Adam sinned God put him in the Garden of Eden "to work it and take care of it." (2:15) As wonderful as the description of the Garden sounds it was not self-maintaining. This shows us that work is not the result of Adam's sin. The part of the curse involving work seems to deal with the frustration we feel when we work. Work is something God created us to do in order to manage His creation. Now, once we understand how special God's creation is and what kind of responsibility we have to be good managers of it, we realize we must work together effectively and constantly depend on God for wisdom and strength. The family unit is uniquely designed to manage God's creation. When we are working together as a family unit we experience God's protection against the hostilities of nature and He provides us with the food and resources we need to live. Inevitably, the picture that comes to mind is a farming family. The husband is out plowing the fields and doing manly work. The wife is cooking, cleaning, canning fruits and vegetables, knitting clothes and doing things for the children. She's doing the "woman's work."

*The Purpose for Sex*

But most of us don't live on a farm. So how are we to apply this business of managing God's creation together if we don't deal directly with the land? There are more gender differences than just physical strength. And the gender differences run so much deeper than merely who has to do the cooking and cleaning and take out the trash. Males and females think differently, approach problems differently, feel differently, etc. Paul says" For the husband is the head of the wife as Christ is the head of the church, his body, of which he is our Savior. Now as the church submits to Christ, so also wives should submit to their husbands in everything." "Husbands, love your wives, just as Christ loved the church and gave himself up for her to make her holy, cleansing her by the washing with water through the word, and to present her to himself as a radiant church, without stain or wrinkle or any other blemish, but holy and blameless. In this same way, husbands ought to love their wives as their own bodies. He who loves his wife loves himself. After all, no one ever hated his own body, but he feeds and cares for it, just as Christ does the church for we are members of his body. For this reason a man will leave his father and mother and be united to his wife, and the two will become one flesh. This is a profound mystery, but I am talking about Christ and the church. However, each one of you also must love his wife as he loves himself, and the wife must respect her husband." When a husband loves his wife with the selfless, unconditional, sacrificial and trustworthy love with which Christ loves us and the church, his wife normally should have no problem at all submitting to him. If she can't, she needs to examine her own self to find out why. Finally, it is the husband's mission in their marriage to lead her to more spiritual maturity so that she reflects God's character more and more beautifully. So the marriage relationship is to serve as a model of the church's relationship with Christ, while the church's relationship with Christ serves as a model for the marriage relationship.

*Save The Family*

This is truly an amazing, beautiful thing and an incredibly powerful weapon against Satan and his rebellious forces.

# PART II

The Homosexuals

# CHAPTER IV

## Not Born. .A Choice

There are, of course, many psychological and physiological factors that would contribute to a male child orienting and identifying himself with homosexuality. There is no direct scientific evidence that homosexuality is inherited although some studies have so indicated. These studies, upon closer investigation, have been refuted as being flawed. So the controversy rages with a lack of conclusive evidence. However, studies have shown there is a relationship, in male homosexuality, with a male child relationship with his parents, and in particular, his father, before the male child became a homosexual. When the male child feels that his father is rejecting him in some way, either outright or by psychological distancing, he fails to identify his own gender. The same holds true when there is no father in the family during the male child formative years. This sense of rejection by a father and/or a son is usually a mutual one, accompanied by a sense of helplessness by both parties. The lack of a healthy relationship of a male child with his father is a strong factor and can't be ignored. This leaves a male child lacking a male role model with which he can identify and as this sense of lack works out in his life as he grows, he seeks a bonding with another male which takes a different, physical and sexual bonding. Studies on young girls who become lesbians seem to be lacking in qualitative depth as most studies on the subject draw their conclusions based upon studies of male homosexuals. **There are a whole range of emotions displayed when the subject of "gay marriages" comes up. There are violent arguments for and against such a legal union. What is it about this subject that draws such vicious attacks and such vicious defense?**

## Save The Family

Some people find homosexuality personally offensive to them. Some state moral and ethical codes which should be considered. Some say that the societal values have always reflected the fact that marriage is a union that can only be consummated by a man and a woman. Anger becomes the basis of this issue simply because the homosexual community wants the world to believe the life is natural and it's "NOT." There are varying definitions and descriptions of what a homosexual is, what a lesbian is and what the term "gay" means. Then there's the subject of bisexuality. It's difficult to realistically utilize these differing terms without arousing a variety of emotions. When the kingdom of GODs principles interject with the subject of "gay people" there is an emotional steam that arises and fogs our vision to such a degree that we can't even see the pot from which it came. If we push heterosexual relationships and marriage to an extreme in our societal values and totally exclude homosexuality from our consideration we then see the results of such an exclusionary societal value and practice. In this heterosexual extreme, men and woman cohabitate and/or marry with a consequent percentage of babies being born. Society continues with the population dying in their old age, but with new babies being born to take the place of older retired and dying citizens. There are a lot of peripheral issues that could be discussed here, but are not within the scope of this discussion. In this broad imaginary overview, if we now push homosexual relationships and marriage to an extreme in our societal values and totally exclude heterosexuality from our consideration we can the results of such an exclusionary societal value and practice. In this homosexual extreme, men cohabitating and/or marrying men or women cohabitating and/or marrying women there would be few, if any, babies born. Any babies from such a union would have to automatically either include adultery with a partner of the opposite sex to impregnate a woman, or artificial insemination.

## Not Born. .A Choice

Society would also continue with the population dying in their old age, but with few, if any, babies are born to take the place of older retired and dying citizens. There are also a lot of peripheral issues that could be discussed here, but are not within the scope of this discussion. If a true exclusively homosexual or lesbian cohabitation and or marriage were practiced, there would be no babies being born and within 100 years there would be no human beings left on this earth. The next societal value to look at is the working dynamics of a marriage. Marriage between a man and a woman involves union in sexual intercourse, which is an important expression of mutual love and also continues to keep our planet populated by the attendant pregnancy and motherhood which accompanies such a union. Unfortunately, there is a problem in our current society in that abortion of these babies has become an item of convenience for irresponsible persons who don't understand that real "choice" must be made *before* engaging in sexual intercourse, not *after* they have become pregnant. This has had a tremendous effect upon our society and economy. Sexual intercourse continues the cycle of humanity on this earth. This expression of mutual love by a man and a woman serves a biological function to create new life. With the arrival of the new baby, a family, i.e., a male husband and a female wife, is then redefined as "baby makes three." As more babies are born to the married male husband and female wife, the family becomes larger. In time the children of this union also marry and continue the procreation process by expressions of love. With more time, there is built up a family unit of mothers and fathers, grandsons and granddaughters, great-grandsons and daughters, uncles, aunts, cousins, birthday celebrations, graduation ceremonies, recognition of wedding anniversaries, establishment of family traditions and etc.

Moral and ethical values will have been formed and redefined and refined and practiced—all built around the mutual love, protection, safety and desirability of the family unit. These values will be incorporated into the cultural values of the contemporary society in which these families live. This is all very basic, that in the sexual union of men and men and women and women, there is no such biological function available. There is no life in such a union, only sensual pleasure. The cycle of continuing humanity doesn't exist. There is no baby; there is no larger family with moral and ethical values being formed, redefined, refined and practiced. There is nothing to contribute to the cultural values of the contemporary society in which these people (not a family) live again; very basic In order to have a baby, adultery and/or fornication may be resorted to. This is not an addition to cultural values, it negates value. Artificial insemination may be utilized, which I understand is not really a very loving physical act in itself. Only with a marriage between a man and a woman can artificial insemination be a source for true loving acts. At this point we have to ask ourselves what we really want as societal values. What is society's approval of a moment of sexual sensual pleasure for its own sake? Is this a loving act     between two men—or between two women? Is there really any purpose in this practice other than pure selfishness? There is obviously no value to morality, ethics or societal values, there is no value in perpetuating the human race. The Family Research Council states that "...   evidence indicates that "committed" homosexual relationships are   radically different from married couples in several key respects:"relationship duration""monogamy vs. promiscuity" "relationship commitment "number of children being raised" "health risks" "rates of intimate partner violence"

## Not Born. .A Choice

Male homosexual relationships last only a fraction of the length of most heterosexual marriages and few homosexual relationships achieve the longevity common in heterosexual marriages. A study of homosexual men in the journal AIDS found that the "duration of steady partnerships" was 1.5 year. Their research indicates that the average male homosexual has hundreds to thousands of sex partners in his lifetime. Homosexual relationships ascribe a radically different meaning to "committed" or "monogamous." Many self-described 'monogamous' couples reported an average of three to five partners in the past year. All couples with a relationship lasting more than five years have incorporated some provision for outside sexual activity in their relationships and view sexual relations outside the relationship to be the norm and adopting monogamous standards as an act of oppression. Sexual relationships are primarily for pleasure rather than procreation. And they are taught that monogamy in a marriage is not the norm and should be discouraged if one wants a good "marital" relationship. Research shows there is a significant difference between the negligible lifetime fidelity rate of 4.5 percent cited for homosexuals and the 75 to 85 percent cited for married couples. This indicates that even "committed" homosexual relationships display a fundamental incapacity for the faithfulness and commitment that is obvious to the institution of marriage. Surprisingly few homosexuals and lesbians choose to enter into legally recognized unions where such arrangements are available, indicating that such couples do not share the same view of commitment as typified by married couples. Data shows in the areas where same-sex unions or marriages were made legal, reveal that only a small percentage of homosexuals and lesbians identify themselves as being in a committed relationship, with even fewer taking advantage of civil unions or, in the case of same-sex "marriage."

*Save The Family*

This indicates that even in the most "gay friendly" localities, the vast majority of homosexuals and lesbians display little inclination for the kind of lifelong, committed relationships that they purport to desire to enter. **As a typical example, 79 percent of homosexuals and lesbians in Vermont choose *not* to enter into civil unions. In Sweden, about 98 percent of Swedish homosexuals and lesbians do *not* officially register as same-sex couples. In the Netherlands, where "gay marriage" is legal, only 2.8 percent of the homosexual and lesbian population has registered their unions as "married." In other words, 97 percent of homosexuals and lesbians in the Netherlands chose *not* to get "married."** Only a small minority of gay and lesbian households have children. Beyond that, the evidence also indicates that comparatively few homosexuals choose to establish households together—the type of setting that is normally prerequisite for the rearing of children. Only a small percentage of partnered homosexual households actually have children. Those that do may include biological children conceived in a previous heterosexual relationship. **The evidence does not support the claim that significant numbers of homosexuals desire to provide a stable home for children. The evidence indicates that homosexual and lesbian relationships are at far greater risk for contracting life-threatening disease compared with married couples. Young gay men have become more likely to contract HIV from a steady sexual partner than from a casual one. Lesbians involved in exclusive sexual relationships also are not at reduced risk for sexual disease. Homosexual and lesbian relationships experience a far greater rate of mental health problems and suicide attempts compared to married couples and non-homosexual peers. Research indicates very high levels of violence in homosexual and lesbian relationships.**

## Not Born. .A Choice

**90 percent of the lesbians surveyed had been recipients of one or more acts of verbal aggression from their intimate partners during the year prior to this study, with 31 percent reporting one or more incidents of physical abuse. The incidence of domestic violence among gay men is nearly double that in the heterosexual population. Surveys conducted by the U.S. Department of Justice confirm that homosexual and lesbian relationships had a far greater incidence of domestic partner violence than opposite-sex relationships including cohabitation or marriage. In addition to the findings from their research the Family Research Council also state they "... present evidence from gay activists themselves indicating that behind the push for gay marriage lies a political agenda to radically change the institution of marriage itself" by pushing the parameters of sex, sexuality, and family, and in the process transforming the very fabric of society as we know it to naturally be.** A former homosexual man explains in an interview why even homosexuals involved in "committed" relationships do not practice monogamy: "In the gay life, fidelity is almost impossible. Since part of the compulsion of homosexuality seems to be a need on the part of the homophile to "absorb" masculinity from his sexual partners, he must be constantly on the lookout for [new partners]. Consequently the most successful homosexual "marriages" are those where there is an arrangement between the two to have affairs on the side while maintaining permanence in their living arrangement." "The evidence is overwhelming that homosexual and lesbian "committed" relationships are not the equivalent of marriage. In addition, there is little evidence that homosexuals and lesbians truly desire to commit themselves to the kind of monogamous relationships as signified by marriage. What remains, then, is the disturbing possibility that behind the demands for "gay marriage" lurks an agenda of undermining the very nature of the institution of mar

Apart from any theological arguments, or any morality arguments, the societal value of "gay marriage" must be measured as a negative value by those who are responsible guardians of our contemporary society. When a man refers to another man as his "wife" or a woman refers to another woman as her "wife," it rattles reality. **What is being tacitly stated is that there is a make-believe "marriage" which, statistically, will be a relationship of short duration, with both people having multiple sexual partners, that any commitment to such a "marriage" is lip-service only to satisfy an unstated heterosexual society code, a horribly artificial and contrived method of incorporating babies into the "marriage" (in those very few instances where children are in such a household), an on-going scenario of mental health problems working themselves out in day to day living, many of which will turn into verbal aggression and domestic violence. And all the while living in a shroud of fear of contracting deadly sexually transmitted diseases, this qualify as an ugly self-deceiving "let's pretend" "fantasy."** Heterosexual unions also have a problem with short term relationships, promiscuous behavior, lack of commitment to the relationship, a rising abortion rate because children are not wanted, mental and physical abuse and domestic violence. Much to our shame, there is also a lack of responsibility in heterosexual marriages and heterosexual cohabitation without marriage. However, positive impact from positive societal values over many centuries puts social and peer pressure upon those who value the role of the family unit as the core of our social values. But with the proliferation of both heterosexual and homosexual relationships impacting society with negative values, the traditional values which our society values are being put at risk of being watered down and polluted so as to be meaningless.

## Not Born. .A Choice

Longevity of relationships, monogamous relationships, lifetime commitments, birthing babies and providing these growing future citizens with a happy and safe domestic family environment, sparing them from situations that cause mental health problems and exposure to deadly sexually transmitted diseases, verbal aggression and domestic violence—these are all important factors for healthy family relationships and for children who are growing up and maturing. Because the liberal media and interests have managed to classify criticisms of the "gay lifestyle" as being "politically incorrect" in the minds of an ignorant and accepting public, it must be realized that something is wrong with the politics and the politicians and other special interest groups who continue to attempt to foster negative social values. Blind acceptance by the public of these logical fallacies puts blame for the state of things as they now see them. These negative social values are also being promoted as being desirable for the heterosexual lifestyle as well by many media outlets. The homosexual or "gay" community is more than glad to add their voice to attempt to impact heterosexual society with negative values. A large percentage of TV series and "specials," popular songs, movies, books, commentaries and newspaper articles reflect that fact. There are many alliances formed by those in the "gay" community and those who oppose traditional society values for the purpose of destroying every trace of the GOD given principles indoctrinated in the Sealed Constitution of these United States of American values in our society. In looking at the statistics and studies and conclusions to be drawn from them, there are several things that should stand out. The majority of the homosexual community is really quite content with their short term, promiscuous, relationships, devoid of any real commitment and avoiding the responsibility of raising children.

They are also well aware of the risks involved in excessive verbal and physical abuse and exposure to deadly sexually transmitted diseases, and the domestic violence. In other words, they are content to "do their thing," with one exception—they want the American privilege to do their thing, in private, without persecution and harassment and being looked down upon as somehow inferior in our society. It could be called a desire for peaceful coexistence. That description, of course, doesn't fit the more radical among them. By the "more radical among them" I mean those members of the "gay community" who blatantly perform sex acts in public places, who dress up as members of the opposite sex, who have surgical procedures to attempt to change their gender, who promote the desirability of having sex with children and who actively pursue especially perverted sexually deviant practices. Marked progress has been made in some quarters of our society in acceptance of the homosexual person as a subculture of our society. Not everyone, of course, falls into that category. There are also radicals among the heterosexual community who would use force against the homosexual community to adapt to and adopt heterosexual societal values and practices. But, a favorable climate for "coming out of the closet" was being felt by many in the homosexual community, because these human beings, like the rest of us, want acceptance of themselves as a person. Admittedly, this is a difficult choice for homosexuals and lesbians to make as it leaves them open and exposed to a lot of things. It's equally as difficult for heterosexuals to "accept" the homosexual lifestyle so "acceptance" has to be modified, if not redefined. "Acceptance" of the homosexual person is established, but with certain limitations in the mind of the acceptor. As this limited acceptance was being felt in some, but not all, levels of heterosexual society, the special interest groups become aware of a new tool, a new weapon that could be used by them to help bring about the demise of the Kingdom of GOD and our principles.

## Not Born. .A Choice

Many in the Homosexual political arena boldly and deceitfully put their plan into action. In particular has whipped an evangelical frenzy to pro-actively force their homosexual lifestyle upon the world. To put it more bluntly, they have become confused and used and abused by many special interest groups under the guide lines of "civil rights" for the homosexual community. In fact, the homosexual community appears to have every right that every other American has. They are free to marry anyone of their choice of the opposite sex. To want to put a law into effect that makes it legal to marry a person of the same sex is not called "civil rights nor is it called "equal rights." That would be a "special human rights, the right to declare being born gay and not a choice to be gay. When the homosexual community switched their tactics from simply attempting to gain a higher degree of acceptance in the heterosexual community, and attempted to prove that homosexual households are remarkably similar to heterosexual married couples and that there is no cultural or moral difference between homosexuality heterosexuality they encountered a resistance they didn't expect. And when many politicians thought that the homosexual community was a greater political force than they are, those same politicians began to hypocritically cater to the homosexual community to gain favor with them. Many, if not most, of those politicians still don't have a clue about how things really work with this complex issue. Why are the politicians so inclined? Because they, the politicians, have bought into the exaggerated lies of those who live the "gay" lifestyle and they think this group makes up 10% or more of the population, which translates in their minds to 10% or more of votes, when, in fact, statistics show they only consist of from one to three per cent of the population. Encouraged by what they thought was political clout, the homosexual community became braver, looking to the more publically known among them to aggressively push the issue under the philosophy that the squeaky wheel gets the grease.

## Save The Family

The spotlight has gone full circle and the homosexual community has had their day, basking in that very short-lived and artificially illuminated minute focus. But under the enlightened intense scrutiny of statistical studies, the whitewash has been flushed away from their attempts to convince society that they, too, measure up to Western civilization and American values and morals. This whitewash was provided by the money interests of the special interest groups who will continue to increase their efforts to stir up the homosexual community to this pretense, and the homosexual community may, or may not; once again rally around their mentors. **The Human Rights Campaign, arguably the country's most powerful lesbian and gay organization, responded to politician Herman Cain's assertion that being gay is a choice. They asked their members to "Tell Herman Cain to get with the times! Being gay is not a choice!" They reasoned that Cain's remarks were "dangerous." "Because implying that homosexuality is a choice gives unwarranted credence to roundly disproven practices such as 'conversion' or 'reparative' therapy. The risks associated with attempts to consciously change one's sexual orientation include depression, anxiety and self-destructive behavior." The problem with such statements is that they infuse biological accounts with an obligatory and nearly coercive force, suggesting that anyone who describes homosexual desire as a choice or social construction is playing into the hands of the enemy.** To the extent to which gay biology had become a moral and political crisis came into full view when an well known actress, after commenting to a <u>New York Times Magazine</u> reporter that she "chose" to pursue a lesbian relationship after many years as a content heterosexual, was met with outrage by lesbian and gay activists.

## Not Born. .A Choice

As one horrified gay male writer proclaimed, "She just fell into a right-wing trap, willingly....Every religious right hatemonger is now going to quote this woman every single time they want to deny us our civil rights." Under considerable pressure from lesbian and gay advocacy groups, the actress recanted her statement a few weeks later, stating instead that she must have been born with bisexual potential. Yes, it's true that straight people are more tolerant when they believe that lesbian and gay people have no choice in the matter. If homosexual desire is hardwired, then no one can cannot change it; many live with this condition, and it would be unfair to judge them for that which they cannot change. By implication, if they *could* choose, of course they would choose to be heterosexual. Any sane person would choose heterosexuality "NOT SO". And when homophobic people come to the opposite conclusion—that homosexual desire is something they *can* choose—then they want to help make the right choice, the heterosexual choice. And they are willing to offer this help in the form of violent shock therapy and other "conversion" techniques. In light of all this, I can absolutely understand why it feels much safer to believe that one is born this way, and then to circulate this idea like their lives depend on it (because, for some people, this truly is a matter of life and death). Indeed, most progressive straight people and most gay and bi people hold the conviction that sexual orientation is natural. They have taken their lead from the mainstream gay and lesbian movement, which has powerfully advocated for this view. But the fact that the "born this way" hypothesis has resulted in greater political returns for gay and lesbian people doesn't have anything to do with whether it is true. Maybe, as gay people, they want to get together and *pretend* it is true because it is politically strategic.

*Save The Family*

That would be interesting. But still, it wouldn't make the idea true. People like to cite "the overwhelming scientific evidence" that sexual orientation is biological in nature. But show the study that claims to have proven this, and I will show you a flawed research design. An even greater problem with the science of sexual orientation is that it seeks to find the genetic causes of gayness, as if we all agree about what gayness is. To say that "being gay" is genetic is to engage in science that hinges on a very historically recent and specifically European-American understanding of what being gay means. In Ancient Greece, sex between elite men and adolescent boys was a common and normative cultural practice. According to historians these relationships were considered the most praise-worthy, substantive and Godly forms of love (whereas sex between a man and a woman was, for all intents and purposes, sex between a man and his slave). If men having frequent and sincere sex with one another are what is meant by "gay," then do you really believe that something so fundamentally different was happening in the Ancient Athenian gene pool? Did some evolutionary occurrence enable Plato's ancestors to seek to get rid of all heterosexual genes? And what about native cultures in which all boys engage in homosexual rites of passage? Is it imagining that one could identify some genetic evidence of propensity to ingest sperm as part of a cultural initiation into manhood? What about all of the cultures around the globe in which male homosexual sex does *not* signal gayness except for under certain specific circumstances (you are only gay if you are the receptive sexual partner, or if you are feminine)? A homosexual couples cannot manage God's creation as effectively for a couple of reasons: First, if those involved are so dead set against God and His wisdom, what reason would they have for even caring about God's creation.

## Not Born. .A Choice

Even most heterosexuals don't care about God's creation for the same reason. They don't care about God or the things of God. Second, the unique physical, emotional, mental and spiritual qualities of men and women aren't there to form a long lasting team. Homosexual relationships don't last long. The more a society breaks down the family, the more resources it must shift to things like fighting crime and achieving physical and mental health. As a result, the society becomes less productive and abuses the environment. Because they lack the complementary natures of male and female, a homosexual couples can not complete each other. In fact, men become sexually oriented toward other men when they have learned to reject the female nature, and women become sexually oriented toward other women when they reject the masculine nature. We know this from sound psychological studies. There is absolutely no evidence of a genetic or biological cause. The few studies that are cited by the activists that suggest the orientation has a genetic cause were done by openly gay men and have been proved to be based on biased research. Homosexuality is caused by unhealthy relationships with family members during childhood. So by the time the person is an adolescent they feel like they have always been that way. But no child is born with a homosexual orientation. It is learned. This is why one must avoid labeling someone as "a homosexual." No one is truly homosexual by nature. All people were created as heterosexual and some have learned to be sexually oriented toward the same sex. But they are still a heterosexual human being whether they feel that way at the time or not. And for that reason the orientation can be unlearned, as so many people do with professional help.

Since the early 1970s, homosexual people have increasingly claimed that they were "born gay" and that, therefore, they could not change even if they wanted to. In the gay community itself more than 90% of gays now believe genes are a significant factor in their orientation—a ten-fold increase in fifty years (1). By repeating this claim over and over again for decades now, they have managed to win over a large percentage of heterosexual "believers" to their cause, without any substantial basis in fact to validate the claim that they were "born that way." "Born gay" is, in fact, a hoax of mammoth proportions that has been accepted by many institutions, organizations and individuals in our culture, even by those in the "Christian church" and even by many apparently "born-again Christians" (1). Therefore, it is necessary to examine carefully the facts concerning the origins and development of homosexuality to see if there is any truth at all to the "born gay" claim. Most of the relevant information can be grouped into three main categories: biological studies, cultural evidence and social factors. The critical question is whether homosexuality is already determined at birth by biological factors and is immutable (unchangeable), or develops later as a result of post-natal experiences and factors, and is fluid (changeable). As you see, the evidence strongly supports the view that homosexuality develops primarily as a result of post-natal experiences and factors, and is fluid (changeable); pre-natal influences (including genetics) have, at most, a weak and non-determinative role. This research has focused primarily on possible genetic contributions to the development of homosexuality but other potential biological factors, such as hormones and brain anatomy, have received considerable attention as well. So, let's first take a look at evidence for genetic causation of homosexuality.

## Not Born. .A Choice

In this regard, it is important to note at the outset that if homosexuality were genetically determined, it would have been bred out of existence in only several generations; it would not exist today. Whereas there was some research in the early 1990s suggesting the existence of a "gay gene", this evidence has since been thoroughly refuted and disproven: there is no "gay gene", and it is now well documented that genetics does not *determine* sexual orientation. Most of the more recent research has focused on the degree to which genetics may *influence* the development of homosexuality, along with other factors. In this regard, the most powerful and conclusive results have come from "twin studies". The results of twin studies have the unique advantage of reflecting the combined influence of all possible, pre-natal, biological factors (genes, hormones, brain morphology and antibodies) on the development of homosexuality. As the design of research studies using identical twins (who both have exactly the same genes) has improved, the reported percentage of homosexual people whose identical twin is also homosexual has declined to only about 10% (by contrast, genetic *determination* of homosexuality would result in nearly 100% of such twin pairs being both homosexual), indicating that there is only a very weak genetic influence on the development of homosexuality. This low level of genetic influence is also the estimated level of genetic influence on virtually any kind of human behavior, which indicates that there is no particularly outstanding influence of genetics on the development of homosexuality. Comparable results and conclusions were obtained for non-identical twins of the same gender.

Such low-level genetic influences on human behavior are known to be non-determinative and treatable by therapy and/or counseling. For instance, the best example to date of a genetically related behavior (mono-amine oxidize deficiency leading to aggression) has shown itself remarkably responsive to counseling. It seems appropriate to conclude, therefore, that there is, at the most, only a very small genetic influence on the development of homosexuality, and that this relatively minor influence can be overcome (nullified) through behavioral therapy, which we know to be a fact. Dean Hamer, one of the main authors of the "gay gene" publications and a self-proclaimed homosexual, summed it up nicely for us: "There will never be a test that will say for certain whether a child will be gay. We know this for certain," this means, as clearly as anyone could state, that no one is "born gay". Concerning other suggested biological causes of homosexuality, there have been presented evidence against a significant role as well, that the differences in brain structure cannot be attributed to pre-natal influences, since there are no discernible structural differences at birth, not even between male and female brains. Major differences do develop during childhood and adolescence, and these differences can be attributed to known post-natal influences. Possible anatomical differences in the brains of mature homosexual men vs. mature heterosexual men can also be attributed to known post-natal influences, as brain anatomy is known to be affected by learning and behavior, even in adults. An examination of the relevant research literature dealing with the possible influence of pre-natal hormones and antibodies on subsequent development of homosexuality, also indicates that these factors play little, if any, role.

## Not Born. .A Choice

In view of the fact that genetics and other pre-natal biological influences have an extremely small effect, if any, on the development of homosexuality, these results clearly support the conclusion, based on results obtained through therapy and counseling, that post-natal, environmental influences have a far greater role in the development of homosexuality than does genetics or other suggested pre-natal influences. There are also several kinds of cultural evidence indicating that homosexuality is not genetically determined, but is, instead, strongly influenced by post-natal events and influences. This evidence was reviewed many researchers. If causation of homosexuality were to be genetically determined, then it would appear in about the same percentage in all cultures, but this is clearly not the case. The prevalence of homosexuality has varied considerably in different cultures. For example, Homosexuality is historically and exceptionally rare in Orthodox Jews. And among the genetically related tribes of the New Guinea Highlands, homosexuality was mandatory among one tribe, practiced by 2-3% of a second tribe and completely unheard of in a third tribe. A significant number of cultures appear not to have practiced homosexuality at all. Moreover, if causation of homosexuality were to be genetically determined, then its occurrence in any given culture would be stable over very long periods of time (1,000 years or more), but in some cultures, homosexuality disappeared within several generations. Anthropologists attribute many such sudden changes to Christian influences, which represent a set of post-natal, non-biological, cultural factors. Researchers have documented numerous examples of adult celebrities and homosexuality advocates who have spontaneously changed from homosexual to heterosexual.

Furthermore, at least six specific examples of adults who changed sexual orientation spontaneously without therapy or counseling have been documented. Homosexuality does not conform to any genetically prescribed model, but does appear to have an overwhelmingly cultural component, ebbing and flowing with changes in cultural values and expectations and with personal experiences. In addition to the cultural influences on the development and practice of homosexuality mentioned, there are several other social factors that are known to have an important role. Researchers pointed out that the percentage of homosexuality in males reared in urban environments is 3.3 times that of males reared in rural environments, while the corresponding factor for homosexuality in females is 2.3 times, indicating a very strong influence of the urban environment in the development of homosexuality. Many found that adults raised by homosexual parents are up to 12 times as likely to self-identify as homosexual or bisexual as are adults raised by heterosexual parents, which indicates that post-natal environmental factors associated with growing up in a homosexual household (such as having homosexual adult role models and unequivocal acceptance of homosexuality) can play a major role in the development of a homosexual orientation. A re-interpretation of results obtained using a research technique called "path analysis" has also shown that post-natal social factors do lead to homosexuality. Two of these studies produced similar results and were found to lend good support to the idea of a constellation of environmental factors influencing the development of homosexuality rather than biological factors. In these studies, environmental factors accounted for 38% of female homosexuality and 76-78% of male homosexuality.

## Not Born. .A Choice

A third study, using a variation on the path analysis approach, showed that one post-natal social factor, gender non-conformity during childhood and adolescence ( sissy-ness or tomboyish-ness), is about 10 times stronger than genetic factors in the development of homosexuality. Some researchers studied same-sex sexual attraction in opposite-sex twins, with unique and relevant results. Adolescent males who are opposite-sex twins are twice as likely as expected to report same-sex attraction, and the pattern of similarity across pairs of same-sex preference for sibling pairs does not suggest genetic influence apart from social influences. Their results support the hypothesis that a post-natal social factor (less gendered socialization in early childhood and pre-adolescence due to the presence of an opposite-sex twin) shapes the subsequent development of same-sex sexual attractions in opposite-sex twins. It was reviewed and summarized some of the published information on religiously mediated and secularly mediated change in sexual orientation from homosexual to heterosexual. Numerous studies have shown that both religiously and secularly mediated change in sexual orientation occurs in highly motivated, dissatisfied homosexuals at a rate that is comparable to the success rates generally achieved by therapists and counselors for psychological disorders and behavioral problems, such as alcoholism. And many studies have found that, for the most part, these are long-term, stable shifts in sexual orientation. In fact, many ex-gays have been happily married with children for several-to-many years. What is the significance of these results relative to the claim that homosexual people are born gay?

First, they confirm that pre-natal influences, including genes, do not *dictate* sexual orientation, because very significant change in sexual orientation has been achieved through therapy and counseling. Such change would not be possible if sexual orientation were fixed at birth. And second, the fact that therapy and counseling are successful at a rate that is comparable to the success rates generally achieved by therapists and counselors for psychological disorders and behavioral problems, such as alcoholism, confirms that any predisposition to homosexuality that may be present at birth is so weak that it can be nullified by subsequent intervention. "As psychoanalysts and psychotherapists, has said quote "we are treating obligatory homosexuality successfully, changing sexual orientation from homosexual to heterosexual. Such a change would be unthinkable if there were any truth at all to the organic or biological or hereditary *causation* of homosexuality."There seems to be some consensus that homosexual people do not choose to have the same-sex attractions and sexual feelings that they experience initially, but that doesn't mean that living a homosexual life-style does not involve choices. Once that first same-sex sexual attraction is encountered, there is a choice as to whether or not to act on it, and the same choice is made every time that attraction is experienced. Bi-sexual people make a choice every time they engage in homosexual sex rather than heterosexual sex. Heterosexual people who are married with children and then forsake their marriage for a homosexual relationship have made a choice to do so. And the fluidity in sexual orientation found especially in lesbians, but also in gays, speaks to the choice of sexual orientation available to many, if not most, homosexual people, at least until their late teens. All things considered, it seems reasonable to conclude that a homosexual *lifestyle* is entirely a matter of **"CHOICE"**.

## Not Born. .A Choice

Since pre-natal factors apparently have very little to do with the development of homosexuality, how, then, can we correctly envision the development of homosexual orientation to answer this question, let's first consider the development of heterosexual orientation. Psychologists are unanimous in their belief that heterosexuality is environmentally, not genetically, determined. No one appears to be born heterosexual. Rather, heterosexual attraction is learned, developing over a period of time in response to certain environmental factors, in particular:

• Good maternal nurture from the earliest stages and through the first few years

• Identification with and imitation of the parent of the same sex

• Acceptance by and identification with same-sex peer groups

• Identification in a boy with what is culturally "masculine" and in a girl with what is culturally "feminine" (this is called "gender conformity").

• The day-in-day-out treatment of boys and girl, as boys or girls, respectively

• The biologically programmed hormonal rush of puberty

- Falling in love

- Culturally prescribed sexual behaviors, such as arousal over women's breasts.

- Personal sexual preferences and behaviors that can be traced back to early sexual arousal in unique circumstances.

It is believed that, for a variety of reasons, homosexuality develops when the normal pattern of heterosexual development is not followed. Reasons include sexual abuse (by men), and a variety of ruptures with same-sex role models. Sometimes this is the father or mother, sometimes peers, probably including siblings. Quite a common consequence is being or feeling less masculine (males) or feminine (females) than others in the same-sex peer group. This can lead to rejection by peers (even other peers who are homosexual) leading to feelings of being different, gender non-conformity and a growing drive to make up the sensed deficit through a strong connection with an individual of the same sex, which becomes eroticized and then manifested as homosexual behavior. Once the pattern of sexual gratification starts, a habit begins, becomes ingrained, and then often addictive. When the process gets to this point, it is very difficult, but not impossible, to effect a change in sexual orientation because the desire for homosexual gratification has become ingrained and extremely powerful. (It is important to note that one gets oneself into this condition through a series of personal choices and decisions made repeatedly over a long period of time; it is not imposed upon him/her by any biological factors, including genes.)

## Not Born. .A Choice

It should not be surprising; therefore, that it will take a series of very difficult personal choices and decisions made repeatedly over a long period of time to achieve a reversal of homosexual orientation and/or behavior, but it is possible; many exclusively homosexual people have managed to do so. Some homosexuality advocates claim that homosexual people are not only born gay, but that *God created them that way* (with same-sex attractions). However, such a claim is diametrically opposed to the biblical witness; there are scriptural proofs that God is not the source of the same-sex attractions and desires that homosexual people experience. First, the Bible clearly and consistently condemns homosexual behavior as sin (Genesis 19:5, Jude 1:7; Leviticus 18:22; Leviticus 20:13; Romans 1:26-27; I Corinthians 6:9-10; and I Timothy 1:10). Now, if God himself were to instill same-sex attractions and desires into homosexual people, then, by doing so, He would be tempting them to sin sexually. However, the Bible also states, emphatically, that God does *not* tempt anyone to sin (James 1:13-14). The necessary conclusion is that God in His Word *would* not create anyone as a homosexual, because to do so would violate His very nature and character, which is to hate sin. And secondly, after God had created Adam and Eve as heterosexual Man & Woman, the Bible says that "God saw all that he had made, and it was very good" (Genesis 1:31). "All that He had made" could not have included homosexuality, because the Bible clearly and consistently condemns homosexual behavior as evil, not good. That — the creation of Adam and Eve – was "the last of the work of creation that God was doing" (Genesis 2:2). It follows, then, that God not only *would* not, but also *did* not, create anyone homosexual. Homosexuality must have first appeared at some later time, after God had finished creating. Since same-sex attractions and desires do not come from God, where do they come from?

The Bible says that sin entered the world through the "original sin" of Adam and Eve (Genesis 3:1-19) *after* the last of the work of creation that God was doing (Genesis 2:2), and that "each person is tempted when they are dragged away by *their own evil desire* and enticed" (James 1:14). Thus, same-sex sexual attraction (homosexuality) is a result of sin entering the world through the disobedience of Adam. Moreover, since God does not put the same-sex urges into homosexual people, it follows that such urges do not constitute a valid argument that God approves of their choice of consequences, namely, homosexual acts. Rather, God's moral laws were given to communicate the sinfulness of our urges (lying, stealing, vengeance, adultery, fornication, and homosexual sex) that are opposed to His will. There is nothing fixed or final about the homosexual orientation and its natural expression, homosexual behavior. No politician, church leader or member, judge, teacher or counselor, or homosexual person, or friend or family of a homosexual person, needs to feel forced into a position on homosexuality based on the apparent immutability of homosexual orientation. Homosexuality is not inborn, not genetically dictated; nor for that matter heterosexuality or any other human behavior. In fact, our genes do not make us do anything. Whether its homosexuality, a foul temper, or addiction to drugs, our genes have very little to do with it. The level of genetic influence could easily be as low as 10%, the balance of 90% coming from *post-natal* cultural and environmental influences. And that 10% is not a direct genetic influence on homosexual orientation; it is a direct influence on a separate trait that can *predispose* toward homosexual orientation. Every human being has a 10% genetic influence on behavior of any kind, and that minimal genetic influence drops commensurately with whatever environmental interventions (cultural influences, social factors, therapy and counseling) of an opposing kind are brought to bear upon it.

## Not Born. .A Choice

So, the next time a homosexuality advocate tries to convince you that homosexual people are born gay, that God made them that way, that their homosexuality is "natural" and/or that their homosexual orientation cannot change, do not accept that. They are operating on a lie, to also get you to believe that lie, as the evidence clearly shows. First, everyone is born into this world with a heart of stone (Ezekiel 11:19 and 36:26) and deaf ears (Deuteronomy 29:3-4). The only ones who can listen to the word of God and believe it are those to whom God has given a "heart of flesh" (Ezekiel 11:19 and 36:26) and "ears to hear" (Isaiah 32:1-4). These are the ones we are able to reach with the truth of God's word; they are our target audience, if you will. We love the others, but we cannot expect them to agree with us unless and until God gives them a "heart of flesh" and "ears to hear". That is God's decision and His work, not ours; Second, those to whom God gives a "heart of flesh" and "ears to hear" will, at some point in the conversion process, become "born again". To be "born again" is not an option for salvation; it is an absolute requirement (John 3:1-8). When one is "born again", God, by the Holy Spirit, replaces their heart of stone with a heart of flesh (Ezekiel 11:19 and 36:26); that is, He removes the old human spirit they were born with, which is at enmity with God, and replaces it with a new human spirit (Ezekiel 11:19 and 36:26), which is from God (John 3:1-8) and in harmony with God. The "born again" person loves the word of God and eagerly believes (receives) it (1 John 4:6). But to those who are not "born again", it is foolishness (1 Corinthians 1:18 and 2:13); we should not expect them to believe it, because in their present condition, they cannot (1 Corinthians 2:13 and 1 John 4:6). To persist in trying to persuade them becomes, at some point, "casting our pearls before swine", and Jesus instructed us not to do that: "Do not give dogs what is sacred; do not throw your pearls to pigs.

If you do, they may trample them under their feet, and turn and tear you to pieces" (Matthew 7:6); and Third, Let us continue to proclaim the truth of God's word for the sake of those who are "born again" and are in the process of being sanctified by the Holy Spirit (that's all of us who are "born again"!). And let us not grow weary in doing this good work (Galatians 6:9) because unbelievers rant and rail against us; they are still at work in the earth doing the work of the devil (1 John 3:8 and Ephesians 2:2), so do not listen to them. The outcome of this "labor of love" of ours is up to God, not us. God only asks us to do our part by continuing to proclaim the truth of His word. He alone will bring forth the fruit of our labor according to His perfect will, His perfect plan and His perfect timing (Galatians 6:9). There are basically three studies that led activists to trumpet the notion that homosexuality is biologically determined. These studies were conducted by a post-mortem examination focusing on a particular cluster of cells in the hypothalamus known as the INAH-3. It was reported that what had been found a "subtle but significant differences" between the brains of homosexual men and the heterosexual men. Research had a number of important limitations, and very little information about the sexual histories of the research participants. Some of the subjects died of AIDS. Although there were differences between experimental and control groups, some presumed heterosexual men had small brain nuclei in the critical area, and some homosexual men had nuclei large enough to be within the normal heterosexual range. Activists proclaimed that the biological roots of homosexuality had been established. But it is important to stress several limitations of the study. First the observations were made on adults who had already been sexually active for a number of years. To make a real compelling case, one would have to show that these nervous system differences existed early in life preferably at birth.

## Not Born..A Choice

Without such data, there is always at least the theoretical possibility that the structural differences are actually the result of differences in sexual behavior perhaps the "use it or lose it" principle. Furthermore, even if the differences in the central area of the brain rise before birth, they might still come about from a variety of causes, including genetic differences, differences in stress exposure, and many others. It is possible that the development of the INAH-3 (and perhaps other brain regions) represent a final common path' in the determination of sexual orientation, a path to which innumerable factors may contribute according to this research. Another limitation arises because most of the gay men whose brains studied died of complications of AIDS. Although some were confident that the small size of INAH-3 in these men was not an effect of the disease, there is always the possibility that gay men who died of AIDS are not representative of the entire population of gay men. For example, they might have a stronger preference for receptive anal intercourse, the major risk factor for acquiring HIV infection. Thus, if one wished, one could make an argument that structural differences in INAH-3 relate more to actual behavioral patterns of copulation than to sexual orientation as such. It will not be possible to settle this issue definitively until some method becomes available to measure the size of INAH-3 in living people who can be interviewed in detail about their sexuality according to research. Further, it's important to stress what wasn't found, it was not proven that homosexuality was genetic, or found any genetic cause for being gay. It didn't show that gay men are born that way, the most common mistake people make when interpreting the researched work. Nor did It locate a gay center in the brain INAH-3 and is less likely to be the sole gay nucleus of the brain than a part of a chain of nuclei engaged in men and women's sexual behavior...Since researching an adults brains, it is not known if the differences found were there at birth, or if they appeared later. The research demonstrated that sexual behavior can actually change brain structure. "These findings give proof that theoretically to know to be the case–that sexual experience can alter the structure of the brain, just as genes can alter it. It is possible that differences in sexual behavior causes (rather than are caused by) differences in the brain. Later, additional clarification regarding biology and homosexuality occurred: Although there are significant differences between the attitudes of lesbians and gay men it is clear that both groups are far more inclined to consider their sexual orientation a biological given than is the general population….Should we take these assertions seriously? Not entirely, according to research. No one even remembers being born, let alone being born gay or straight. When a gay man, for example, says he was born gay he generally means that he felt different from other boys at the earliest age he can remember. Sometimes the difference involved sexual feelings, but more commonly it involved some kind of gender non comfort or sex traits-disliking rough and tumble play for example, that were not explicitly sexual. These differences, which have been verified in a number of ways, suggest that sexual orientation is influenced by factors operating very early in life, but these factors could still consist of environmental factors such as parental treatment in the early postnatal period. The biology of homosexuality, noted, "…people who think that gays and lesbians are born that way are more likely to support gay rights."The next focused was on identical twins, non-identical twins, non-adopted siblings and adopted siblings. In this example, 56 set of identical twins and 54 sets of non-identical twins. There was found a 52% concordance rate for the identical twins which means that for every homosexual twin, the chances were about 50% that his twin would also be homosexual.

## Not Born. .A Choice

For non-identical twins, the rate was about 22%, showing that about 1 in 5 twins who were homosexual had a homosexual brother also. For non-twin brothers, the concordance rate was 9.2%. Interesting enough, it was found that the concordance rate in adopted brothers was 11.2%. The most fascinating question, however, is that if there is something in the genetic code that makes an individual homosexual, why did not all of the identical twins become homosexual since they have the exact same genetic endowment? One researcher provided some comparative data on twin studies. The concordance rate for identical twins on measures of extroversion is 50%, religiosity is 50%, divorce is 52%, racial prejudice and bigotry is 58%. From another research study, one has to conclude that environmental influences play a strong role in the development of homosexuality. The third study, and perhaps the most sensationalized of the three studies since it emerged at the time of the controversy surrounding gays in the military during the Clinton era, was conducted. This group attempted to link male homosexuality to a stretch of DNA located at the tip of the X chromosome, the chromosome that some men inherit from their mothers. In one study, it examined 40 pairs of non-identical gay brothers and asserted that 33 pairs–a number significantly higher than the 20 pairs that chance would dictate–had inherited the same X-linked genetic markers from their mothers. Criticism of one's research came from a surprising source: A scientist at Yale University School of Medicine who invented the method used, suggest that their results are consistent with X-linkage because maternal uncles have a higher rate of homosexual orientation than paternal uncles, and cousins related through a maternal aunt have a higher rate than other types of cousins. However, neither of these results is statistically significant."

It was assumed the environment also played a role in sexual orientation, as it does in most, if not all behaviors. Homosexuality is not purely genetic environment plays a role. There is not a single master gene that makes people gay...we will ever be able to predict who will be gay. Citing the failure of research, furthermore, "The pedigree failed to produce what it was originally hoped to find. In fact, there was never a single family in which homosexuality was distributed in the obvious pattern that was observed in a pea plants." What is more intriguing is that when the study was replicated with research that was more robust, the genetic markers were found to be no significant. "It is unclear why our results are so discrepant from original study. Because one study was larger than that of another study, certainly had adequate power to detect a genetic effect as large as reported in that study. Nonetheless, one's data do not support the presence of a gene of large effect influencing sexual orientation at position XQ 28. When, a *Times* reporter asked, whether this theory ruled out social and psychological influences, the response was "Absolutely not, ...from twin studies which already knew that half or more of the variability in sexual orientation is not inherited. One research studies try to pinpoint the genetic factors, not to negate the psychosocial factors," "Recent studies postulate biologic factors as the primary basis for sexual orientation, However, there is no evidence at present to substantiate a biologic theory, just as there is no evidence to support any singular psychosocial explanation. While all behavior must have an ultimate biologic substrate, the appeal of current biologic explanations for sexual orientation may derive more from dissatisfaction with the current status of psychosocial explanations than from a substantiating body of experimental data. Critical review shows the evidence favoring a biologic theory to be lacking.

## Not Born. .A Choice

In alternative model, temperamental and personality traits interact with the familial and social surroundings as the individual's sexuality emerges. Because such traits may be heritable or developmentally influenced by hormones, the model predicts apparent non-zero heritability for homosexuality without requiring that either genes or hormones directly influence sexual orientation *per se*." Independently, noted that credible evidence is lacking for a biological model of homosexuality. They conclude that "human sexual orientation is complex and diversely experienced and that a bio-psychosocial model best fits the current state of knowledge in the field." So what does all of this mean about biology and the genesis of homosexuality? Critical reviews of the studies attempting to link biology and homosexuality, and subsequent acknowledgments by the researchers themselves, yield only one conclusion: biology alone is insufficient to explain the development of homosexuality. Any reputable scientist, regardless of which side of the political debate he or she embraces, when asked whether homosexuality is nature or nurture, must answer "yes." What is fascinating is that more than 50 % of the scientists who report research in this area are self-identified as gay or lesbian. This is disproportionate to the 2-3% (The Kinsey myth that 10% of the population is homosexual has been thoroughly discredited) which is the current estimate of the number of homosexual men and women in the population. The developmental biologist from Brown University, "Dr. Anne Fausto-Sterling, a self-identified lesbian, offers some interesting insight." Referring to the "born that way" argument, she states: It provides a legal argument that is, at this moment, actually having some sway in court. For me, it's a very shaky place. Its bad science and bad politics, it seems to me that the way we consider homosexuality in our culture is an ethical and a moral question.

When asked about how much of her thinking about change in sexuality comes from her own life, Fausto-Sterling responded, My interest in gender issues preceded my own life changes. When I first got involved in feminism, I was married. The gender issues did to me what they did to lots of women in the 1970s: they infuriated me. My poor husband, who was a very decent guy, tried as hard as he could to be sympathetic. But he was shut out of what I was doing. The women's movement opened up the feminine in a way that was new to me, and so my involvement made possible my becoming a lesbian. My ex and I are still friends. It is true I call myself as lesbian now because that is the life I am living, and I think it is something you should own up to. At the moment I am in a happy relationship and I don't ever imagine changing. Still, I don't think loving a man is unimaginable. So if biology is insufficient to explain the development of homosexual attraction, what does the research say about the developmental or environmental factors? Homosexual population is not a homogenous population. There are likely different routes that lead to a homosexual attraction, a homosexual orientation or a homosexual identity. Not only do the processes appear to be different for men and women but a homosexual attraction does not necessarily lead to a homosexual orientation. And not all homosexually oriented people claim a homosexual identity. Gender nonconformity is the single most common observable factor associated with homosexuality. One researcher puts it: "Most sissies grow to be homosexuals, and most gay men were sissies as children…despite the provocative and politically incorrect nature of that statement, it fits the evidence. In fact, it may be the most consistent, well-documented, and significant finding in the entire field of sexual orientation research and perhaps in all of human psychology."

## Not Born. .A Choice

In his own study, he asked the following questions: "Did you consider yourself less masculine than other boys your age, or were you ever regarded as a sissy as a child?" The answer was yes for 68% of the gay men compared with 5% of the straight men. Another question, "Did you enjoy sports such as baseball and football as a child? Of the gay men, 8% said very much compared to 78% of heterosexual men said very much. The gay men recalled substantially more gender atypical behaviors than the heterosexual men." Another researcher noted that "…gays and lesbians were more nonconformist than heterosexuals in the following gender-differentiated traits:"

- Participation in rough and tumble play (RPT), competitive athletics, or aggression
- Toy and activity preference
- Imagined roles and careers (significant difference for men only)
- Cross-dressing
- Preference for same or opposite sex playmates

Social reputation as a sissy or tomboy

As concluded that homosexual women were more likely than heterosexual women to report having been extreme tomboys as children. These researchers reported that 70% of homosexual women recalled being "boy-like" in childhood compared to 16% of heterosexual women. The research data is extensive in correlating gender non-conformity and later self-identification as homosexual. Another area where there has been substantial research is the area of sexual abuse. Which concluded that:

- homosexually-assaulted males identified themselves as subsequently homosexual seven times as often as the non-assaulted group.

- the mean age at which the molestation was reported was 18.2 with a range of 15 to 24.

- the age at the time of the molestation ranged from 4 to 16 with a mean age of 10.

of an extension group, one half of the victims currently identified themselves as homosexual and often linked their homosexuality to their sexual victimization experiences. It is found that gay males are more likely than heterosexual males to become sexually active at a younger age (12.7 vs. 15.7). In clinical settings, homosexual men frequently report an early introduction to sexuality. Researchers with 942 non-clinical adults (97% of the men and women were participating in a gay-pride celebration). Gay men and lesbian women reported a significantly higher rate of childhood molestation than did a comparison group of heterosexual men and women. Forty-six per cent of the gay men in comparison to 7% of the heterosexual men reported homosexual molestation. Twenty-two per cent of the lesbian women in comparison to 1% of the heterosexual women reported homosexual molestation. So did the molestation contribute to the identification as gay or lesbian in adulthood? The question is particularly intriguing because 68% of the men and 38 % of the women did not identify as gay or lesbian until after the molestation. Another area where there has been considerable research is peer abuse. As boys, many homosexual men report name-calling, feeling rejected, being excluded by their peers. An activist theorist from Cornell, offers an interesting theory of how homosexuality develops. His theory is referred to as EBE or the Exotic Becomes the Erotic.

His theory is that boys feel attraction for those who were different from them. The theory basically proposes that biological variables, such as genes, prenatal hormones, and brain neuroanatomy, do not code for sexual orientation *per se* but for childhood temperament that influences a child's preference for sex-typical or sex-atypical activities and peers. These preferences lead children to feel differently from same-sex peers-to perceive themselves as dissimilar, unfamiliar, and exotic. This, in turn, produces heightened nonspecific autonomic arousal that subsequently gets sexualized or eroticized in that same class of dissimilar peers: exotic becomes erotic. In essence, temperamentally sensitive boys sexualize that with which they are not familiar. A Psychiatrist that has done significant work in this area has concluded, he strongly support the role of peer abuse as a factor in the development of gender confusion and later, homosexuality. A final area of developmental factors is associated with family relationships. In homosexual men there appears to be a disconnect between them and their fathers as well as an over connect with them and their mothers. The psychoanalytic literature seems to hold true in many case where there is a perception of the father being distant, uninvolved and un-approving. Many clinicians report that fathers have a difficult time connecting with their gender atypical sons. A researcher concluded that the relationship of the child to the father may be more critically predictive of outcome than any other aspects of the relationship with the mother. In a study that found that 72% of the homosexual men recalled feeling very little or not at all like their fathers. So what does all of this mean? Regarding homosexuality, there are simply no variables that are by themselves, totally predictive. What was known is that the probable genesis of homosexuality lies in a combination of temperament and environmental factors such as sexual abuse and peer abuse along with familial factors.

Leaving aside this etiologic discussion, the next question is homosexuality immutable? Is it fixed, or is it fluid and amenable to change? There is a fairly good body of research that demonstrates that homosexuality is more fluid than fixed. Research suggests that some kind of changes occurred for many who now identify as ex-gay. A study by, a professor at the University of Utah, concluded that sexual identity is far from fixed in women who are not exclusively heterosexual. A renowned Canadian researcher admits the lack of evidence for the biologic theory of homosexuality offers an interesting observation. Referring to those on both sides of the debate, the politically and ideologically conservative and "rightist" as well as the politically and ideologically liberal and "leftist," he noted that both sides agree that homosexual orientation is "more fluid than fixed." "At times," as noted, "there really is something to the expression that science and politics make strange bedfellows." Perhaps the most significant study completed to date was conducted by Robert L. Spitzer. Against tremendous protest and politics of intimidation, the study was published in the prestigious *Archives of Sexual Behavior*. Ironically enough, Spitzer was the psychiatrist who led the charge to remove homosexuality as a disorder from the psychiatric manual in 1973. Spitzer is a self identified secular humanist atheist Jew who has been consistent in his support of gay rights. Briefly, Spitzer conducted a study of 200 people who reported that they had changed from homosexual to heterosexual. Spitzer found that 66% of the men and 44% of the women who had participated in therapy to change their homosexual orientation had arrived at what he called "good heterosexual functioning." Additionally, 89% of the men and 95% of the women reported that they were bothered slightly or not at all, by unwanted homosexual feelings. In Spitzer's own words:

## Not Born. .A Choice

"Like most psychiatrists I thought that homosexual behavior could be resisted, but sexual orientation could not be changed. I now believe that's untrue-some people can and do change." Spitzer concluded that the changes occurred not just in behavior but in core features of sexual orientation.[41] In a commentary published last year, Dr. Scott Hershberger, a scientist from the University of California at Long Beach, a long time supporter of gay rights and a self-identified essentialist (a individual who believes that homosexuality is biologically determined), reviewed the Spitzer research. Instead of just commenting on the Spitzer research, he elected to conduct a Guttmann Scalability analysis. Basically, this is a mathematical test used to determine whether or not the reported changes occur in a cumulative, orderly fashion. His conclusion, "The orderly, law-like pattern of changes in homosexual behavior, homosexual self-identification, and homosexual attraction and fantasy observed in Spitzer's study is strong evidence that reparative therapy can assist individuals in changing their homosexual orientation to a heterosexual orientation. Now it is up to those skeptical of reparative therapy to provide comparably strong evidence to support their position. In my opinion, they have yet to do so." While it is beyond the scope of this lecture to talk about the theory and methods that are helpful in diminishing homosexual attractions, perhaps I can offer a very simple statement with which most therapists in this area would agree. The basic theory is that social and emotional variables affect gender identity which in turn determines sexual orientation. The work of the therapist is to help individuals understand their gender development. Subsequently such individuals are able to make choices that are consistent with their value system. The focus of treatment is to help individuals fully develop their masculine or feminine gender identity. Homosexuality is not normal.

On the contrary it is a challenge to the norm...Nature exists whether academics like it or not. And in nature, procreation is the single relentless rule. That is the norm...Our sexual bodies were designed for reproduction...No one is born gay. The idea is ridiculous...homosexuality is an adaptation, not an inborn trait. Is the gay identity so fragile that it cannot bear the thought that some people may not wish to be gay? Sexuality is highly fluid, and reversals are theoretically possible. However, habit is refractory, once sensory pathways have been blazed and deepened by repetition-a phenomenon obvious with obesity, smoking, alcoholism or drug addiction–helping gays to learn how to function heterosexually, if they wish is a perfectly worthy aim. We should be honest enough to consider whether or not homosexuality may not indeed, be a pausing at the prepubescent stage where children band together by gender....Current gay cant insists that homosexuality is not a choice; that no one would choose to be gay in a homophobic society. But there is an element of choice in all behavior, sexual or otherwise. It takes an effort to deal with the opposite sex; it is safer with your own kind. The issue is one of challenge versus comfort

# CHAPTER V

## Civil Rights or Humanly Wrong

Many politicians are equating legal rights for homosexuals with the black struggle against racism. This is not a valid argument. There is a specter haunting America. It is the movement to promote and legalize homosexual marriage. The movement has adopted a cunning political strategy to appeal to everyone from the suburban soccer mom to the urban white-male liberal: It has packaged its demand for radicalizing and the redefining of marriage in the rhetoric and imagery of the U.S. civil rights movement. This strategy, though truly cynical and possibly racist, has enormous strategic purposes. For what reasonable and fair-minded American would object to a movement that conjures up images of Martin Luther King Jr. along with pacifist marchers facing down unleashed attack dogs and men with fire hoses? In the aftermath of that struggle for racial justice, who today is prepared to risk being branded a bigot for opposing the homosexual's activist agenda? This strategy is the most brilliant plan of utilizing the race card since the days of the "Civil Rights" movement. We have not witnessed so brazen a misuse of African-American history for partisan purposes since the "poverty pimps" of more than 35 years ago—who leveraged the American public's sense of guilt and fair play in order to hustle affirmative action set-asides. But the partisans of homosexual marriage have a problem. There is no evidence in the historical graphical literature of the civil rights movement or in the movement's struggle against slavery to support their political and moral argument of moral equivalent. For it was in the crushing experience of slavery that the civil rights movement was born.

## Save The Family

As one black historian observed more than 30 years ago the black American experience as a function of slavery is unique and without analogue in the history of the United States. ***Though other ethnic and social groups have experienced discrimination and hardship, none of their experiences historically and politically can compare with the physical brutality of slavery.*** The civil rights movement was born with the establishment of the Continental Congress of these United States as a slaveholding republic. This extraordinary history included the kidnapping and brutal transport of blacks from African shores, being stripped of their language, identity and culture in order to subjugate and exploit them in a slave buyer market hosted by the European Nations. It included the constitutional enshrining of these evils in the form of a U.S. Supreme Court decision—Dred Scott v. Sandford—which denied blacks any rights that whites had to their respect. It included the establishment of the Jim Crow culture and *de jure* racial discrimination after the Dred Scott case was overturned by a civil war and three historic constitutional amendments. ***It is these basic, historical facts that weaken the efforts of homosexual-marriage apologists to exploit civil rights movement as a way to advance the interest of a generalized privileged community. In fact, the campaign for homosexual marriage is ironically an assertion of white female privilege. Frequently, same-sex couples wanting to marry are white lesbians seeking the accoutrements of family life, including kids and the proverbial white picket fence, while excluding the benefit of a father for the children. From their positions of socio-economic privilege, they insist that their desires must be viewed as rights instead of preferences. The dominant demographic behind this political initiative is neither homosexual males nor people of color—notwithstanding the occasional interracial lesbian couple that is portrayed for propaganda purposes.***

## Civil Rights or Humanly Wrong

*It is precisely the indiscriminate promotion of various social groups' desires and preferences as rights that has gutted the moral authority of the pale liberal civil rights industry. Let us consider the question of rights. What makes a homosexual's aspiration to overturn thousands of years of universal recognition of morality and practice a "Right"? Why should an institution designed for the reproduction of civil society and for the rearing of children in a moral environment be refashioned to accommodate relationships integrated around basic non-marital conduct? One must, address directly the assertion of "discrimination." The claim that the definition of marriage as a union between one man and one woman constitutes discrimination is based on a false analogy with statutory prohibitions on interracial marriages in many states during much of the 20th century. This alleged analogy collapses when one considers that skin pigmentation is utterly irrelevant to the procreative and unitize functions of marriage. Racial differences do not affect or interfere with the ability of sexually complementary of spouses becoming "one flesh" through sexual intercourse that fulfills the behavioral conditions of procreation as GOD so ordained. The law of marital consummation makes it clear that this bodily union serves as the foundation of the profound sharing of life at every level—biological, emotional, dispositional, rational and spiritual. This Divine Ordained form of life-sharing explains not only why marriage can only be between a man and a woman, but also why marriages cannot be between more than two people.* Moreover, the alleged analogy also disregards the fact that the whole point of those prohibitions was to maintain and advance a system of racial subordination and exploitation. It was to maintain a caste system in which one race was relegated to conditions of social and economic inferiority.

## Save The Family

The definition of marriage as the union of a man and a woman does not establish a sexual caste system or regulate one sex to conditions of social and economic inferiority. It does, to be sure, exclude the lawful recognition of "marriages" formed from some types of sexual combining—including polygyny (more than one partner), polyandry, polyamory and same-sex relationships. However, there is nothing discriminatory about laws that decline to treat all sexual wants as morally equal. *People* are equal in worth and dignity, but **sexual choices and lifestyles are not**. That is why the law's refusal to license polygamous, polyamorous and homosexual unions is entirely right and proper. In recognizing, favoring and promoting true marriage, the law does not violate the "rights" of people whose "lifestyle preferences" are denied the stamp of legal approval. Rather, it furthers and fosters the common good of civil society, and makes proper provision for the physical and moral protection and nurturing of children. The word "discrimination" has now been emptied of its normative and historical content—thereby serving to disadvantage blacks in American society. Members of any group, however privileged, now can simply claim the term and launch their own personalized civil rights industry. It is the revival of a culture of narcissism. Defending the civil rights legacy likely will be a cold comfort to its historical advocates because the loss of its distinctive nature is our own fault. It is our failure, philosophically and politically, to develop a compelling historical movement that has contributed to its decline and decay. From the teaching in school to the use of the term "civil rights" in the public square, the notion of *civil* rights has been diluted and nearly emptied of its content in relation to the historical experience of blacks people in these United States of America.

Civil Rights or Humanly Wrong

*That the authorized institutional inheritors of the civil rights movement failed to recognize and prevent this loss, brings into question their ability to continue as effective leaders of the black community.* It is especially sad and disturbing that the established leadership of the civil rights industry has utterly failed to resist the corrupting and co-opting by a mostly white special-interest group of the history of the civil rights phase of the black freedom struggle such as the "NAACP" taking on new membership of the homosexual community simply because the black community alienated the organization based on its lack of credibility in this country and abroad. This failure highlights the need for a regime change in favor of new leadership, as well as a post-civil rights conceptual framework for addressing a more complex racial reality. Moreover, in light of the phenomenon of judicially mandated homosexual marriage, *we believe that our called black leaders hosting the titles of "Bishop, Pastor, Preacher, Minister and most of all Reverend need to speak forcefully in favor of a federal marriage amendment to the GOD Given Principle Sealed indoctrinated Constitution of these United States of America.* If their support for true marriage alienates them from their Caucasian business friends, so be it. No community has suffered more than has the black community from the weakening of marriage at the hands of purveyors of the doctrines of the sexual revolution. It is black sons and black daughters who have paid the bulk of the cost imposed by a cultural elite that seeks to overthrow biblical and societal principles of sexual restraint and responsibility. Leaders of the black community should therefore be in the vanguard of the movement to prevent further moral erosion and begin reversing historical declines.

## Save The Family

We respectfully suggest that Martin Luther King Jr. did not give his life, nor Fannie Lou Hamer her struggle, so that those could be free to pursue their polygyny forms of sexuality under the banner of the black civil rights movement. A gay-marriage advocate explained to a reporter that marriage is a civil matter, not a church affair. Those who want church weddings can have them, but marriage is a matter of civil law. And since it is unconstitutional to deny equal civil rights to citizens, it is unconstitutional to deny to homosexual couples the right to marry. At this important moment in the U.S. debate over same-sex "marriage" and the likelihood of a long campaign to try to add a marriage amendment to the Indoctrinated GOD Given Principle Sealed Constitution of these United States of America, it is important to evaluate the grounds of the arguments. In particular, we need to be clear about what constitutes a civil right. It is certainly true that the contention over marriage is about civil law. Marriage law has long been a state matter, and in the United States that has meant, literally, a state rather than a federal matter. In any case, the law has until now taken for granted that marriage is an institutional bond between a man and a woman. Moreover, marriage is something people of all faiths and no faith engage in. Churches, synagogues, and mosques may bless marriages but they do not create the institution. In that sense the question of marriage is not first of all a religious matter in the sense in which most people use the word "religion." **It is ordained by GOD!!!!**

## Civil Rights or Humanly Wrong

However, to insist that the question of marriage is a matter of civil law and not first of all a religious matter does not take us very far. After all, the argument is about what government *ought to do* about keeping or changing the legal definition of marriage. The debate is not between husbands and wives *within* the bond of traditional marriage—like a court case over divorce and child custody. No, this debate is about whether the law that now defines marriage as itself good or bad, right or wrong. And to join that debate one must appeal, by moral argument, to grounds that transcend the law as it now exists. In that regard, the question of marriage is not about a civil right at all. It is about the nature of reality and interpretations of reality that precede the law. Those who now argue that same-sex couples should be included, as a matter of civil right, within the legal definition of marriage are appealing to the ***Indoctrinated GOD Given Principle Sealed Constitution of these United States of American*** principles of equal protection and equal treatment. But this is entirely inappropriate for making the case for same-sex "marriage." To argue that the ***Indoctrinated GOD Given Principle Sealed Constitution of these United States of American*** guarantees equal treatment to all citizens, both men and women, does not say anything about what constitutes marriage, or a family, or a business enterprise, or a university, or a friendship. An appeal for equal treatment would certainly not lead a court to require that a small business enterprise be called a marriage just because two business partners prefer to think of their business that way. Nor would equal treatment of citizens before the law require a court to conclude that those of us who pray before the start of auto races should be allowed to redefine our auto clubs as churches. The simple fact is that the civil right of equal treatment cannot constitute social reality by declaration.

*Save The Family*

Civil rights protections function simply to assure every citizen equal treatment under the law depending on what the material dispute in law is all about. Law that is just must begin by properly recognizing and distinguishing identities and differences in reality in order to be able to give each its legal due. One kind of social relationship that government recognizes, for example, is a free contract by which two or more parties agree to carry out a transaction or engage in some kind of activity. Let's say you contract with me to paint your house. The law of contract does not define ahead of time what might be contracted; it simply clarifies the legal obligations of the contracting parties and the consequences if the contract is broken. Governments and lawyers and the law do not create the people, the business, and the desire to do business. The point is that even in contract law, the law plays only a limited role in the relationship. The law encompasses the relationship only in a legal way. If someone wants to argue that two people who have not in the past been recognized as marriage partners should now be recognized as marriage partners, one must demonstrate that marriage law (not civil rights law) has overlooked or misidentified something that it should not have been overlooked or misidentified. Since the Foundation of the Earth, marriage law has been and continues to be an enduring bond between a man and a woman that includes sexual intercourse—the kind of act that can (but does not always) lead to the woman's pregnancy. A homosexual relationship, regardless of how enduring it is as a bond of loving commitment, does not and cannot include sexual intercourse leading to pregnancy, the creation of "LIFE" that GOD intended. Thus it is not marriage. The much disputed question of whether same-sex relationships are morally good or bad healthy or unhealthy is not the point of legal consideration. The point is about identity and difference.

## Civil Rights or Humanly Wrong

This is the material legal matter of properly recognizing and identifying what exists and distinguishing between marriages and auto clubs, between schools and banks, between friendships and multinational corporations. It has nothing to do with civil rights. To recognize in law the distinct character of a marriage relationship, which entails sexual intercourse, involves no discrimination of a civil rights act against those whose bonds do not include sexual intercourse. Those who choose to live together in life-long homosexual relationships; or brothers and sisters who live together and take care of one another; or two friends of the same sex who are not sexually involved but share life together in the same home—all of these may be free to live as they do, and they suffer no civil rights discrimination by not being identified as marriages. There is no civil rights discrimination against an eight-year-old youngster who is denied the right to enter into marriage. There is no civil rights discrimination being practiced against a youngster who is not allowed the identity of a college student because she is not qualified to enter college. There is no civil-rights discrimination involved when the law refuses to recognize my auto club as a church. A marriage and a homosexual relationship are two different kinds of relationships and it is a misuse of civil rights law to use that law to try to blot out the difference between two different kinds of things. But there is civil-rights discrimination when the White Homosexual Community practices the same ill mistreatments towards the black homosexual community as to what the relationship has been since the days of the "Civil Rights Movement." It is sadden that the "NAACP" would take in the Homosexual Community for simple membership purposes due to the black community lack of membership. Such practice is not fair to either community.

## Save The Family

Those who want homosexual relationships to be redefined as marriages say that many aspects of their relationships are like marriage—having sexual play, living together, loving one another, etc.—and therefore they should be allowed to call their relationships marriages and should be recognized in the law as marriage partners. But this cannot be a proper legal matter until the empirical case has been made that a homosexual partnership and a marriage are indistinguishable. Otherwise, the appeal amounts to nothing more than a request that homosexual partners be allowed to call themselves what they want to call themselves regardless of the differences that exist in reality. The answer they want is for law making and adjudicating authorities to change the law based on the principle that reality is defined by the will and declarations of individuals, all of whom should be treated without discrimination. But here, you see, is the sleight of hand. The appeal now being made for homosexual marriage rights is not an appeal for judges and lawmakers to reconsider past empirical judgments about similarities and differences between heterosexual and homosexual relationships. Rather, it is an appeal for judges and lawmakers to ignore those distinctions in order not to deny citizens the right to call things what they want to call them. It is a version of an appeal for the protection of free speech, and in this case it is a demand that the speech of particular persons to carry the authority to define the structure of reality without regard to the basis of past legal judgments. The antidiscrimination principle is appealed to not in order to show that some married couples have previously been denied the recognition of their marriage. Rather the antidiscrimination principle is being used to ask that no citizen be denied the right to call something what he or she wants to call it.

## Civil Rights or Humanly Wrong

If homosexual relationships are, in this manner, legally recognized as marriages, no realities will change. Heterosexual marriage partners will still be able to engage in sexual intercourse and potentially procreate children; homosexual partners will still not be able to engage in such intercourse. Pregnancy will still be possible only by implanting a male sperm in a female egg, whether that is done by sexual intercourse inside or outside of marriage, or by in vitro fertilization, or by implanting male sperm in the uterus of a woman not married to the man whose sperm are being used. The only thing that will change is that the law will mistakenly use the word "marriage" to refer to two different kinds of sexually intimate human relationships. If this happens, we will need to pay close attention to the consequences. Judges and public officials will then be required to recognize as a marriage any sexually Intimate bond between two people who want to call themselves married. Which means that there will no longer be any basis for distinguishing legally between a heterosexual union and a homosexual relationship. Which means henceforth that there will be no legal basis for restrictions against a homosexual couples obtaining children in any way they choose, for such restrictions would constitute discrimination. And it will mean that when a mature mother and son, or father and daughter, or trio or quartet of partners come to the courts or to the marriage-license bureau to ask that their sexually active relationship be recognized as marriage, there will be no legal grounds *of a non-arbitrary kind* to reject the requests. Because if it is now arbitrary and unjust to recognize heterosexual marriage as something exclusive and different from homosexual relationships, then it will be arbitrary and unjust not to grant the request of other partners to call their sexually intimate and enduring relationships marriage.

## Save The Family

But, of course, since legal declarations cannot turn reality into something it cannot become, a variety of conundrums, contradictions, and anomalies will inevitably arise. And the only way to resolve them will be to revise the law so it squares with, and does justice to, reality. If that is, anyone is interested in crafting the law to do justice to reality. Unlike race, gender, age, ethnicity or religion, sexual orientation is not a protected characteristic under current federal civil rights law. But following the 1969 <u>Stonewall riots of gays in Greenwich Village</u>, a key goal of the gay and lesbian political movement has been to win civil rights protection against discrimination in employment, housing, and elsewhere. Too often, gay men and lesbians face hostility, discrimination -- and sometimes deadly violence -- solely because of their sexual orientation. <u>Hate crimes</u> committed against gays, lesbians, bisexuals, and/or transgendered individuals constitute the third-highest category of hate crimes reported to the FBI -- 14% of all hate crimes reported nationally, according to the <u>Human Rights Campaign</u>. And while violent crime rates have been declining generally, the National Coalition of Anti-Violence Programs reports that the number of actual or suspected anti-gay murders is on the rise: from 14 in 1997 to 33 in 1998 and 28 in 1999. Earlier studies by the <u>National Gay and Lesbian Task Force Policy Institute</u>, including an analysis of 21 different local surveys between 1980 and 1991, found widespread discrimination across the country against gay men and lesbians. According to the report as many as 44 percent of respondents in some cities reported employment discrimination as a result of their sexual orientation. Thirty-two percent reported discrimination in renting a housing unit. The study also said that gay men and lesbians reported discrimination in public restaurants and in receiving health services, obtaining insurance and in education.

## Civil Rights or Humanly Wrong

Legislative attempts to enact anti-bias laws protecting gay men and lesbians have occurred at the federal, state and local level. In Congress, the effort to enact equal protection laws, including coverage for gay men and lesbians, has been underway since 1975, when Rep. Bella Abzug, D-N.Y., introduced the first lesbian and gay civil rights bill. Since then, 12 states and the District of Columbia have enacted laws barring job discrimination on the basis of sexual orientation. The <u>Human Rights Campaign</u> also reports that 23 states and the District of Columbia have enacted state hate crime laws that include protections against violence motivated by sexual orientation bias. The gay rights struggle opened another front during the 1992 presidential election when then-nominee Bill Clinton promised to lift the ban on gays in the military. When Clinton renewed his promise after winning the election, he was met by a storm of protest from both Congress and the military, especially the Joint Chiefs of Staff. In the end the president settled for a compromise that pleased virtually no one. On July 19, 1993, President Clinton announced what he called an "honorable compromise," a "don't ask, don't tell" policy, under which potential recruits would not be asked their sexual orientation, would have to keep that orientation private and not engage in any homosexual conduct and would require the military to curtail its investigation of suspected homosexuals and lesbians. Gay men or lesbians who let their identity be known or who act on their sexuality would still be discharged from the Armed Forces. Similarly, President Clinton's support for Congress' enactment of the Defense of Marriage Act ("DOMA"), which enables states to refuse to recognize same-sex marriages performed in other states, also drew fire from civil rights advocates.

On the other hand, the Clinton Administration made several important regulatory changes, including issuing an executive order banning discrimination based on sexual orientation in all civilian federal workplaces, as well as an executive order prohibiting sexual orientation and other forms of discrimination by federally conducted education programs; and granting asylum for gay men and lesbians facing persecution in other countries. To date, the Supreme Court has decided relatively few cases directly involving gay issues. In Bowers v. Hardwick (1986), the Court upheld Georgia's state law making sodomy a crime. The Court said that constitutional rights to privacy did not encompass what it called "homosexual sodomy," and that the law served a legitimate state interest, namely promoting what the court defined as "majority sentiments about ... morality." Ten years later in Romer v. Evans, on the other hand, the Court struck down as unconstitutional a Colorado state referendum approving an amendment to the state constitution that would have overturned local anti-bias laws. The Court held that the referendum was motivated by irrational bias against gays and lesbians and served no legitimate government interest, thus violating basic federal constitutional guarantees of equal protection.But in Boy Scouts of America v. Dale (2000), the Court dealt civil rights advocates another setback, ruling that the Boy Scouts' First Amendment rights of free expression and association would be violated by enforcement of New Jersey's state law barring sexual orientation discrimination to prohibit them from dismissing a gay Scoutmaster. Current legislative efforts to protect the civil rights of gay, lesbian, bisexual, and transgendered individuals include the Employment Nondiscrimination Act (ENDA), which would prohibit job discrimination on the basis of sexual orientation.

Civil Rights or Humanly Wrong

The Local Law Enforcement Enhancement Act (formerly known as the Hate Crimes Prevention Act) has been another priority; this legislation would extend federal hate crimes jurisdiction to reach, for the first time, certain violent hate crimes committed because of the victim's sexual orientation, gender, or disability, as well as expand current federal jurisdiction over hate crimes committed on the basis of race, national origin, and religion. But in Boy Scouts of America v. Dale (2000), the Court dealt civil rights advocates another setback, ruling that the Boy Scouts' First Amendment rights of free expression and association would be violated by enforcement of New Jersey's state law barring sexual orientation discrimination to prohibit them from dismissing a gay Scoutmaster. Current legislative efforts to protect the civil rights of gay, lesbian, bisexual, and transgendered individuals include the Employment Nondiscrimination Act (ENDA), which would prohibit job discrimination on the basis of sexual orientation. The Local Law Enforcement Enhancement Act (formerly known as the Hate Crimes Prevention Act) has been another priority; this legislation would extend federal hate crimes jurisdiction to reach, for the first time, certain violent hate crimes committed because of the victim's sexual orientation, gender, or disability, as well as expand current federal jurisdiction over hate crimes committed on the basis of race, national origin, and religion. TULSA, Okla. — **Oklahoma** lawmaker Sally Kern, who once called homosexuality "the biggest threat our nation has, even more so than terrorism or Islam," decried a federal judge's ruling striking down the state's ban on **same-sex marriage**. "Homosexuality is not a civil right, it's a human wrong," Kern told KOTV. "Homosexuals are saying, 'This is who we are. This is how we're born.'

## Save The Family

You tell a lie long enough, people start to believe it," she said. In his ruling Tuesday January 12 2014, U.S. District Judge Terence Kern (no relation to Sally Kern) described Oklahoma's ban on same-sex marriage as "an arbitrary, irrational exclusion of just one class of Oklahoma citizens from a governmental benefit." Rep. Sally Kern was joined by members of Oklahoma's congressional delegation, who blasted the ruling as overreaching and disappointing. U.S. Rep. Mark Wayne Mullin, a Republican, said Oklahoma's constitution "protects the sovereignty of states, and with today's ruling, that right has clearly been violated." U.S. Rep. James Lankford, another Republican, said the ruling is an example of "why the American people are so frustrated with government and government officials; the people speak clearly but elected officials and judges ignore them." Also weighing in was The Most Reverend Paul Coakley, the archbishop of the Catholic Archdiocese of Oklahoma City, <u>who said he was "profoundly disappointed"</u> in the ruling, and said it "thwarts the common good." " Not a Civil Right...A Human Wrong"!! Homosexuality is just plain wrong. I base my position primarily on my Christian faith (more on that later), but for all the secular humanists out there, who are so enamored of the god called science, I also base my position on physical, empirical, verifiable fact: male bodies weren't made to go together, nor were female bodies. And if there are so many lesbians (and there are) saying, "I don't need a man," why do they become mannish or date mannish women? So many lesbians dress like men, wear their hair like men, act like men, talk like men, and so many homosexual men (who "don't need a woman") act like women, dress like women, wear their hair like women, talk like women—if you don't need someone of the opposite gender, then why do you bother becoming like the opposite gender, or date such people?

# Civil Rights or Humanly Wrong

The *Times* also makes the uneducated claim that courts were created to rule on the constitutionality of laws. No, actually, they weren't. When the Founders were setting up our nation's government, certain of them made sure that the establishment of courts was for the sole purpose of declaring whether alleged actions were in accordance with written law, and these men also strictly opposed the concept of "judicial review." If someone did something, and that act was deemed by law enforcement officials to be in violation of the law, and the individual took their case to court, the court's job was to determine whether their act (or acts) broke the law. That was it. That was all that courts were supposed to do. It wasn't until later on, in the U.S. Supreme Court case *Marbury v. Madison* in 1803, that the Court, *against the will of the Founders*, enacted the unfortunate precedent of judicial review, whereby courts now have the final say on every law that comes before them. In the wake of Prop 8, there's been a lot of talk from the homosexual community about civil rights—specifically, that marriage of any type is a civil right, and that civil rights should be off-limits to the decisions of voters, and, therefore, that Prop 8 should never have been allowed (and, since it was allowed, should now be thrown out). Advocates of the homosexual community have even compared their plight to that of blacks struggling for civil rights in the '60s. All this talk of civil rights on the part of homosexuals, though, and the comparing of their situation to the black civil rights movement, is unfounded. First, blacks were routinely segregated—separate bathrooms, water fountains, schools—and denied the right to vote, and knocked over with fire hoses; none of this is happening to homosexuals. So for them to be comparing their "plight" to that of blacks in the 1960s is absurd, preposterous, and insulting to blacks. When we talk of civil rights, what we're speaking of is political rights.

For example, the Bill of Rights outlines the fundamental political liberties that citizens of this free country have, liberties that keep government from becoming tyrannical and oppressing its people: If you don't like a certain politician or political party, you have the civil (political) right to vote them out of office; if you dislike something the government is doing, you have the civil (political) right to peacefully protest; if the government tries to tell you who or how to worship, you have the civil (political) right to refuse and to worship as you see fit. In other words, civil rights are all about checks and balances between the government and the people, about ensuring that things stay honest between the two. This is what made the black civil-rights movement a civil-rights movement; they had previously been denied the political freedoms due every American, such as the right to vote, and thus had a legitimate civil-rights argument: To deny them, for example, the right to vote was to treat them unequally under the law. This is the true meaning of the phrase "equal treatment under the law." Homosexuals, on the other hand, are not being denied such rights. Relationships, unlike voting, etc., have nothing to do with protecting citizens from political tyranny. Furthermore, if relationships are classified under the "equal treatment under the law" rubric, then it becomes impossible to objectively draw the line as to which relationships qualify for "equal treatment." What right would any of us have, for example, to deny a 16-year-old the "right" to be with a 21-year-old? Who are any of us to say that such a relationship is not valid? 16-year-olds are people too, right? They have feelings, don't they? Can't they be "in love"? Marriage has nothing to do with civil rights. Marriage is a religious and social issue, something that has nothing to do with keeping government off our backs. Thus, it is an issue whose fate is in the hands of the people.

## Civil Rights or Humanly Wrong

Second, the color of your skin is amoral—that is, it has nothing to do with morality—whereas sexual activity has a lot to do with morality. There is disagreement as to whether homosexuality is genetic; I will here give homosexuals the benefit of the doubt (even though no "gay gene" has been discovered and thus cannot be said empirically to exist), but it doesn't affect my point, which is this: whether genetic-based or learned, homosexual activity (unlike skin color) is a *behavior*, and since the realm of behavior is where morality resides (e.g., is it moral or immoral to engage in such-and-such a behavior?), what homosexuals are asking of society is to enshrine as a civil right a certain behavior—one that many of us find immoral. This is what made the black civil-rights movement a civil-rights movement; they had previously been denied the political freedoms due every American, such as the right to vote, and thus had a legitimate civil-rights argument: To deny them, for example, the right to vote was to treat them unequally under the law. This is the true meaning of the phrase "equal treatment under the law."Homosexuals, on the other hand, are not being denied such rights. Relationships, unlike voting, etc., have nothing to do with protecting citizens from political tyranny. Furthermore, if relationships are classified under the "equal treatment under the law" rubric, then it becomes impossible to objectively draw the line as to which relationships qualify for "equal treatment." What right would any of us have, for example, to deny a 16-year-old the "right" to be with a 21-year-old? Who are any of us to say that such a relationship is not valid? 16-year-olds are people too, right? They have feelings, don't they? Can't they be "in love"? Marriage has nothing to do with civil rights. Marriage is a religious and social issue, something that has nothing to do with keeping government off our backs. Thus, it is an issue whose fate is in the hands of the people.

Second, the color of your skin is amoral—that is, it has nothing to do with morality—whereas sexual activity has a lot to do with morality. There is disagreement as to whether homosexuality is genetic; I will here give homosexuals the benefit of the doubt (even though no "gay gene" has been discovered and thus cannot be said empirically to exist), but it doesn't affect my point, which is this: whether genetic-based or learned, homosexual activity (unlike skin color) is a *behavior*, and since the realm of behavior is where morality resides (e.g., is it moral or immoral to engage in such-and-such a behavior?), what homosexuals are asking of society is to enshrine as a civil right a certain behavior—one that many of us find immoral. It is true that a lot of our civil rights involve behaviors—voting, protesting, worshiping—but you'd be hard-pressed to find anyone who believes that those behaviors are immoral, because they're not. On the other hand, there are a great many people who view homosexual behavior as immoral, and thus it is ridiculous, from our point of view, that such behavior, in the context of "same-sex marriage" or even "civil unions," should be honored as a protected civil right. Of course, most homosexuals see nothing immoral about their sexual behavior, but they need to remember that many people do. So to have homosexuals asking people such as myself to grant civil-right status to what I view as immoral behavior would be like me asking my countrymen to confer civil-right status on something that most of *them* find objectionable, such as stealing. I may think stealing is okay, but that doesn't make it so. I may have even been born with a genetic compulsion to steal, but that still wouldn't make it *right* for me to steal—it would help me to understand *why* I steal, but it wouldn't make my stealing moral, and it wouldn't mean I'd have a basic civil right to have my stealing protected under law.

## Civil Rights or Humanly Wrong

Furthermore, there are many things in human genetics that exist but aren't supposed to, such as physical ailments and mental illnesses. It is clear that these things are abnormal, and we fight to overcome them—we search for cures, we use medicine, counseling, and various therapies. And it is clear, based on (if nothing else) the picture our physiology paints, that homosexuality, whether genetic or chosen, is abnormal. We have each been given a conscience, which is the mediator of our morality. All of us, myself included, face a variety of situations each day in which we must make a choice concerning how we're going to behave—opportunities to steal or leave be, to hit someone with whom we're angry or to resist, to be rude or polite. Many of these things could even be said to be impulses ... but that doesn't make them okay to do. I may have a bad temper, or a penchant for being a crotchety jerk, or a passion for pleasure that knows no bounds ... but having an impulse for any of these doesn't legitimize acting on them. In one of his Townhall columns, titled "Jack Black, Jesus and Prop 8," Frank Pastore raises an intriguing issue, one about which there is much confusion and that's often used against Christians. I'm talking about the Old Testament prohibition against shellfish. I know: earth-shattering stuff, right? Not on its own, it's not, but it's become a famous talking point for homosexual advocates, believe it or not. Whenever anyone such as myself brings up the Old Testament prohibitions against homosexual activity, homosexual advocates often rebut with something like this: "Well the Old Testament also bans the eating of shellfish, but you eat shellfish, right?" Well, first of all, no, I don't eat shellfish. I think they're disgusting. But that's beside the point. Yes, many Christians eat shellfish but oppose homosexuality. So they're big fat hypocrites, right? No. And here's why:

In the course of early human history, everyone had become alike in the sense that everyone did whatever they wanted to do, in rebellion against God and how *He* wanted us to live. So God, in order to teach mankind His ways, began a process of sanctification, which is a fancy way of saying "setting us apart"—making us like Him, making us different from the world. But since we humans can be quite blockheaded, God decided to take things slowly and teach us one bit at a time. One of the key strategies He used was to teach us spiritual truth through object lessons, using everyday material things that the ancient Israelites had easy access to. One such thing was the animal kingdom, so God used animals to teach the Israelites the difference between holiness (spiritual cleanliness) and unholiness (spiritual uncleanliness). And here's where the shellfish come in. Shellfish are bottomfeeders. They eat off the ocean floor, where lots of germy stuff settles. Thus they represented unholiness (spiritual uncleanliness). So God told the Israelites to avoid eating shellfish (and that they *could* eat regular fish, which *aren't* bottomfeeders), and thus gave them a tangible demonstration of how to live the *spiritually* clean life God wanted them to live. (As a side note: God used other animals this way, telling the Israelites, for example, to not eat scavenger birds, because they ate things that had been long dead and thus represented spiritual uncleanliness). So it's not that God was declaring shellfish to be evil and forever avoided; it was simply an object lesson during the early portion of mankind's *gradual* process of spiritual growth. When Jesus was on Earth, He declared that it wasn't what went *into* the body that defiled a person, but what came *out* of a person's heart that caused defilement—thus implying that every kind of food was acceptable for eating.

## Civil Rights or Humanly Wrong

This was confirmed after His Ascension when the Apostle Peter had a vision of a sheet containing several types of animals that Jews considered unclean, but God told him, "What God has cleansed you must not call common" (Acts 10:9-16). This was God's way of telling Peter that Gentiles were welcome in His kingdom, and, I think, another way of God saying, "It's not about the food." And now we come to homosexuality, which, unlike shellfish, was not merely an object lesson. As I've said, Jesus confirmed that there was nothing inherently wrong with shellfish, and that God really was okay with us eating them after all, that He'd only been using them to demonstrate a spiritual lesson. *But God never used this strategy in regards to human sexuality.* From the very beginning of the Bible (Adam and Eve) to the very end of it (Revelation's picture of Jesus as the groom and the Church as His bride), God makes clear His one and only intention for human sexuality: that of one man and one woman in a lifelong commitment (which we call "marriage"). He never gave His approval to polygamy (not even in the case of Solomon), or to adultery (David got in big trouble for that), or to any other sexual relationship besides "one man/one woman" marriage. Not even to homosexuality. And yes, I know (as many homosexuals have lovingly told me) that Jesus never said anything specific against homosexuality. Then again, He never said anything specifically against child molesting, either, but I'm sure we all know what he thinks about *that*. Jesus, however, did have some things to say about human sexuality in general, and what he said is telling. First, during one of his many conversations with his adversaries, he told them, "Have you not read (in the law) how from the beginning God created them male and female?" To me, this is Jesus's way of saying, "Duh, people. Isn't it obvious?

Male and female go together; nothing else does." Second, Jesus was clear that fornication was unacceptable to God ... and fornication is defined as any sexual relationship outside the bonds of marriage ... and the Bible clearly demonstrates that marriage is between one man and one woman ... so by speaking against fornication, Jesus is speaking against *every* type of sexual relationship outside "one man/one woman" marriage—including bestiality, adultery, pedophilia, polygamy, and, yes, homosexuality. The Rev. (and I use that term loosely) Susan Russell of All-Saints Episcopal Church in Monrovia, Calif., said some while back: "The United States is founded on values of freedom of religion and from religion." Actually, "reverend," "freedom from religion" is nothing but a fanciful idea dreamed up by atheists and the ACLU (the Anti-Christian-Liberties Union). Like "separation of church and state," it's a phrase found nowhere in our nation's founding documents. Besides that, no one can be free from religion; even if you don't subscribe to an "organized" religion, you subscribe to whatever *un*organized hodgepodge you decide upon throughout the course of your life. In other words, you believe *something*, and whatever it is you believe, *that* is your religion. Russell went on to say: "All-Saints is part of a national group that believes God's laws include everyone and that the United States Constitution provides protection for everyone." Well, duh. Of course the Constitution applies equally to everyone—but it doesn't say anything about marriage (or abortion, for that matter). And true equality doesn't mean equal results; it means having equal protection of our basic civil (political) rights, and we all have that. You can disagree with any decision, but a decision not in your favor doesn't mean that your basic rights have been violated.

## Civil Rights or Humanly Wrong

And it's funny that Russell speaks of God's laws applying to everyone, because she glaringly fails to encourage obedience to one of His fundamental teachings: that He designed marriage as a particular thing, to the exclusion of all other things, as a way of demonstrating to us the differences and similarities between Himself and humans, and His desire (despite our differences) for intimacy with us. God is clear in his displeasure with homosexuality, as is nature. If you have disagreement with these, then on what do you base your disagreement? Love? The world doesn't know what true love is. True Love came to us 2,000 years ago and we nailed him to a cross. The world wouldn't know love if it stared it in the face. And if *your* definition of love was the one standard, the be-all and end-all, then what of one man and several women who say they "love" each other? And what of the 23-year-old woman and the 16-year-old boy who say they "love" each other, and that their relationship is "consensual"? Just as most people recognize the obvious truth that adults shouldn't be having sex with children, it should be just as obvious that two males or two females don't go together. This entire issue is ridiculous. I've heard a few people say that same-sex marriage should never have come before voters; they're right, it shouldn't have—because the proper sexual relationship between the sexes should be as clear as day, and unnatural behaviors should be left to the darkness, from whence they come and where they belong.

That said, gay marriage is simply not on par with the black civil rights struggle. Not even close. When a group of mostly black protesters stood before the Supreme Court to defend traditional marriage last week, some pundits and social-media commentators wondered how people who once fought for their own civil rights could deny them to others. For one, these black protesters were Christian. Many American Christians are opposed to gay marriage, and people of faith have as much a place in this debate as anyone else. It is amusing how liberals who preach "diversity" are always surprised when it produces frictions or contradictions, which many on the left found last week in black Americans who oppose gay marriage. But for these African-American followers of Christ, there were no contradictions. Race isn't everything. I have gay friends who are married. The states in which they reside might not recognize their unions, but their friends and families do, and they generally live their lives in peace. No one is turning water hoses on them. They are not being attacked by police dogs. There is no Bull Connor or Ku Klux Klan. They are not being lynched en masse, drinking at separate fountains, or being ordered to the back of the bus. This is not to say that gay Americans who wish to have the full benefits of marriage afforded to heterosexual couples don't face adversity. That's a major part of the current debate. But it is to say that any hardship they face can't compare to what black Americans faced 50 or 150 years ago. There have been instances during the gay-rights movement that arguably could be compared to the black civil rights struggle, like the Stonewall riots of the 1960s or Matthew Shepard murder in 1998. Suicides and other problems related to public attitudes about homosexuality have also unquestionably been a horrible ordeal.

Still, with the possible exception of the mistreatment of Native Americans, there has been nothing quite like the systematic exploitation and institutional degradation experienced by earlier black Americans. My purpose here is not to belittle the fight for gay marriage, only to note that those who keep attempting to draw a reasonable comparison to the struggle of African-Americans are in many ways belittling the black experience in the United States. There is a specter haunting America. It is the movement to promote and legalize homosexual marriage. The movement has adopted a cunning political strategy to appeal to everyone from the suburban soccer mom to the urban white-male liberal: It has packaged its demand for the radical redefining of marriage in the rhetoric and imagery of the U.S. civil rights movement. This strategy, though utterly cynical and possibly racist, has enormous strategic utility. For what reasonable and fair-minded American would object to a movement that conjures up images of Martin Luther King Jr. along with pacifist marchers facing down unleashed attack dogs and men with fire hoses? In the aftermath of that struggle for racial justice, who today is prepared to risk being branded a bigot for opposing the homosexual's activist agenda? This strategy is the most brilliant playing of the race card in recent memory. We have not witnessed so brazen a misuse of African-American history for partisan purposes since the "poverty pimps" of more than 35 years ago—who leveraged the American public's sense of guilt and fair play in order to hustle affirmative action set-asides. But the partisans of homosexual marriage have a problem. There is no evidence in the historiographical literature of the civil rights movement or in the movement's genesis in the struggle against slavery to support their political and moral argument of equivalence.

For it was in the crucible of the unique experience of slavery that the civil rights movement was born. As the eminent historian Eugene D. Genovese observed more than 30 years ago, the black American experience as a function of slavery is unique and without analogue in the history of the United States. Though other ethnic and social groups have experienced discrimination and hardship, none of their experiences historically and politically can compare with the physical brutality of slavery. The civil rights movement was born with the establishing of the United States as a slaveholding republic. This extraordinary history included the kidnapping and brutal transport of blacks from African shores and the stripping from them of their language, identity and culture in order to subjugate and exploit them. It included the constitutional enshrining of these evils in the form of a U.S. Supreme Court decision—Dred Scott v. Sandford—which denied to blacks any rights those whites had to respect. It included the establishment of Jim Crow culture and *de jure* racial discrimination after the Dred Scott case was overturned by a civil war and three historic constitutional amendments. It is these basic, historical facts that weaken the efforts of homosexual-marriage apologists to exploit civil rights rhetoric as a way to advance the interest of a generally privileged group. In fact, the campaign for homosexual marriage is ironically an assertion of *white* privilege. Frequently, same-sex couples wanting to marry are white lesbians seeking the accoutrements of family life, including kids and the proverbial white picket fence, while excluding the benefit of a father for the children. From their positions of socioeconomic privilege, they insist that their desires must be viewed as *rights* instead of preferences.

## Civil Rights or Humanly Wrong

The dominant demographic behind this political initiative is neither homosexual males nor people of color—notwithstanding the occasional interracial lesbian couple that is portrayed for propaganda purposes. It is precisely the indiscriminate promotion of various social groups' *desires and preferences* as rights that has eviscerated the moral authority of the paleoliberal civil rights industry. Let us consider the question of rights. What makes a homosexual's aspiration to overturn thousands of years of universally recognized morality and practice a "right"? Why should an institution designed for the reproduction of civil society and for the rearing of children in a moral environment be refashioned to accommodate relationships integrated around intrinsically nonmarital conduct? One must, in the current discussion, address directly the assertion of "discrimination." The claim that the definition of marriage as the union of one man and one woman constitutes discrimination is based on a false analogy with statutory prohibitions on interracial marriages in many states during much of the 20th century. This alleged analogy collapses when one considers that skin pigmentation is utterly irrelevant to the procreative and unitive functions of marriage. Racial differences do not affect or interfere with the ability of sexually complementary spouses to become "one flesh" through sexual intercourse that fulfills the behavioral conditions of procreation. The law of marital consummation makes it clear that this bodily union serves as the foundation of the profound sharing of life at every level—biological, emotional, dispositional, rational and spiritual. Advertisement This complementary form of life-sharing explains not only why marriage can only be between a man and a woman, but also why marriages cannot be between more than two people.

Moreover, the alleged analogy also disregards the fact that the whole point of those prohibitions was to maintain and advance a system of racial subordination and exploitation. It was to maintain a caste system in which one race was relegated to conditions of social and economic inferiority. The definition of marriage as the union of a man and a woman does not establish a sexual caste system or regulate one sex to conditions of social and economic inferiority. It does, to be sure, exclude the lawful recognition of "marriages" formed from some types of sexual combining—including polygyny, polyandry, polyamory and same-sex relationships. However, there is nothing invidious or discriminatory about laws that decline to treat all sexual wants or proclivities as morally equal. *People* are equal in worth and dignity, but *sexual choices and lifestyles* are not. That is why the law's refusal to license polygamous, polyamorous and homosexual unions is entirely right and proper. In recognizing, favoring and promoting true marriage, the law does not violate the "rights" of people whose "lifestyle preferences" are denied the stamp of legal approval. That is why the law's refusal to license polygamous, polyamorous and homosexual unions is entirely right and proper. In recognizing, favoring and promoting true marriage, the law does not violate the "rights" of people whose "lifestyle preferences" are denied the stamp of legal approval. Rather, it furthers and fosters the common good of civil society, and makes proper provision for the physical and moral protection and nurturing of children. The word "discrimination" has now been emptied of its normative and historical content—thereby serving to disadvantage blacks in American society. Malcontented members of any group, however privileged, now can simply invoke the term and launch their own personalized civil rights industry.

## Civil Rights or Humanly Wrong

It is the revival of a culture of narcissism. Defending the civil rights legacy likely will be a cold comfort to its historical advocates because the loss of its distinctive nature is our own fault. It is our failure, philosophically and politically, to develop a compelling historiography of the movement that has contributed to its decline and decay. From the teaching in school to the use of the term "civil rights" in the public square, the notion of *civil* rights has been diluted, a historicized and nearly emptied of content in relation to the historical experience of blacks in this country. That the authorized institutional inheritors of the civil rights movement failed to recognize and prevent this loss brings in question their ability to continue as effective leaders of black people. It is especially sad and disturbing that the established leadership of the civil rights industry has utterly failed to resist the corrupting and co-opting by a mostly white special-interest group of the history of the civil rights phase of the black freedom struggle. This failure highlights the need for a regime change in favor of new leadership, as well as a post-civil rights conceptual framework for addressing a more complex racial reality. Moreover, in light of the phenomenon of judicially mandated homosexual marriage, we believe that black leaders need to speak forcefully in favor of a federal marriage amendment to the Constitution. If their support for true marriage alienates them from their white liberal friends, so be it. No community has suffered more than has ours from the weakening of marriage at the hands of purveyors of the doctrines of the sexual revolution. It is our sons and our daughters who have paid the bulk of the cost imposed by cultural elite that seeks to overthrow societal and biblical principles of sexual restraint and responsibility. Leaders of our community should therefore be in the vanguard of the movement to prevent further moral erosion and begin reversing historical declines.

## *Save The Family*

We respectfully suggest that Martin Luther King Jr. did not give his life, nor Fannie Lou Hamer her struggle, so that libertines could be free to pursue their polymorphous forms of sexuality under the banner of the black civil rights movement.

# CHAPTER VI

## Sodom and Gomorrah

The biblical account of Sodom and Gomorrah is recorded in Genesis chapters 18-19. Genesis chapter 18 records the Lord and two angels coming to speak with Abraham. The Lord informed Abraham that "the outcry against Sodom and Gomorrah is so great and their sin so grievous." Verses 22-33 record Abraham pleading with the Lord to have mercy on Sodom and Gomorrah because Abraham's nephew, Lot, and his family lived in Sodom. Genesis chapter 19 records the two angels, disguised as human men, visiting Sodom and Gomorrah. Lot met the angels in the city square and urged them to stay at his house. The angels agreed. The Bible then informs us, "Before they had gone to bed, all the men from every part of the city of Sodom — both young and old — surrounded the house. They called to Lot, 'Where are the men who came to you tonight? Bring them out to us so that we can have sex with them.'" The angels then proceed to blind all the men of Sodom and Gomorrah and urge Lot and his family to flee from the cities to escape the wrath that God was about to deliver. Lot and his family flee the city, and then "the LORD rained down burning sulfur on Sodom and Gomorrah — from the LORD out of the heavens. Thus he overthrew those cities and the entire plain, including all those living in the cities..." In light of the passage, the most common response to the question "What was the sin of Sodom and Gomorrah?" is that it was homosexuality. That is how the term "sodomy" came to be used to refer to anal sex between two men, whether consensual or forced.

*Save The Family*

Clearly, homosexuality was part of why God destroyed the two cities. The men of Sodom and Gomorrah wanted to perform homosexual gang rape on the two angels (who were disguised as men). At the same time, it is not biblical to say that homosexuality was the exclusive reason why God destroyed Sodom and Gomorrah. The cities of Sodom and Gomorrah were definitely not exclusive in terms of the sins in which they indulged. Ezekiel 16:49-50 declares, "Now this was the sin of your sister Sodom: She and her daughters were arrogant, overfed and unconcerned; they did not help the poor and needy. They were haughty and did **detestable** things before me..." The Hebrew word translated "detestable" refers to something that is morally disgusting and is the exact same word used in Leviticus 18:22 that refers to homosexuality as an "abomination." Similarly, Jude 7 declares, "...Sodom and Gomorrah and the surrounding towns gave themselves up to **sexual immorality** and **perversion**." So, again, while homosexuality was not the only sin in which the cities of Sodom and Gomorrah indulged, it does appear to be the primary reason for the destruction of the cities. Those who attempt to explain away the biblical condemnations of homosexuality claim that the sin of Sodom and Gomorrah was inhospitality. The men of Sodom and Gomorrah were certainly being inhospitable. There is probably nothing more inhospitable than homosexual gang rape. But to say God completely destroyed two cities and all their inhabitants for being inhospitable clearly misses the point. While Sodom and Gomorrah were guilty of many other horrendous sins, homosexuality was the reason God poured fiery sulfur on the cities, completely destroying them and all of their inhabitants. To this day, the area where Sodom and Gomorrah were located remains a desolate wasteland.

# Sodom and Gomorrah

Sodom and Gomorrah serve as a powerful example of how God feels about sin in general, and homosexuality specifically. People find what they want in the Bible. If one looks hard enough, he can find "biblical" support for reincarnation, Eastern religions, Jesus as a guru, divorce for any reason, and flying saucers. Every cult of Christianity uses the Bible to validate its claims and so does some of the occult. It's not surprising, then, that a recent trend in biblical scholarship holds that a careful reading of Genesis in its historical context offers no solid basis to conclude that the destruction of Sodom and Gomorrah had anything to do with homosexuality. This view may seem far-fetched to biblical conservatives, but it is taken very seriously in academic circles. It represents a significant challenge to the rank-and-file Christian who finds in the Genesis account a straight-forward condemnation of homosexual behavior. My goal is to answer that challenge. I have no interest to malign, name-call, offend, attack, bash, belittle, or in any way demean a group of people. I want to determine one thing only: Why did God destroy these two cities? Did it have anything to do with homosexuality itself? In short, what was the sin—or sins—of Sodom and Gomorrah? Though the context of the account in question begins in Genesis 18:16 during God's conversation with Abraham by the Oaks of Mamre, the details of the encounter at Sodom itself are found in Genesis 19:4-13: Before they lay down, the men of the city, the men of Sodom, surrounded the house, both young and old, all the people from every quarter; and they called to Lot and said to him, "Where are the men who came to you tonight? Bring them out to us that we may have relations with them." But Lot went out to them at the doorway, and shut the door behind him, and said, "Please, my brothers, do not act wickedly.

Now behold, I have two daughters who have not had relations with man; please let me bring them out to you, and do to them whatever you like; only do nothing to these men, inasmuch as they have come under the shelter of my roof." But they said, "Stand aside." Furthermore, they said, "This one came in as an alien, and already he is acting like a judge; now we will treat you worse than them." So they pressed hard against Lot and came near to break the door. But the men reached out their hands and brought Lot into the house with them, and shut the door. And they struck the men who were at the doorway of the house with blindness, both small and great, so that they wearied themselves trying to find the doorway. Then the men said to Lot, "Whom else have you here? A son-in-law, and your sons, and your daughters, and whomever you have in the city, bring them out of the place; for we are about to destroy this place, because their outcry has become so great before the Lord that the Lord has sent us to destroy it. "What was the sin of Sodom and Gomorrah? Why did God destroy the two cities? The traditional view is that homosexuality was the principle offense ("Please, my brothers, do not act wickedly"). Yale historian John Boswell offers four possible reasons for the destruction of Sodom: (1) The Sodomites were destroyed for the general wickedness which had prompted the Lord to send angels to the city to investigate in the first place; (2) the city was destroyed because the people of Sodom had tried to rape the angels; (3) the city was destroyed because the men of Sodom had tried to engage in homosexual intercourse with the angels...; (4) the city was destroyed for inhospitable treatment of visitors sent from the Lord. John Boswell thinks that explanation (2) "is the most obvious of the four," though it's been "largely ignored by biblical scholars."Boswell expands on explanation (4), the one he seems to favor as most consistent with "modern scholarship" since 1955:

## Sodom and Gomorrah

Lot was violating the custom of Sodom...by entertaining unknown guests within the city walls at night without obtaining the permission of the elders of the city. When the men of Sodom gathered around to demand that the strangers be brought out to them, "that they might know them," they meant no more than to "know" who they were, and the city was consequently destroyed not for sexual immorality, but for the sin of inhospitality to strangers. Englishman D. Sherwin Bailey also argues this way in *Homosexuality and the Western Christian Tradition*. The men of Sodom wanted to interrogate Lot's guests to see if they were spies. The sin of gang rape was also in view, not homosexuality. In a broader sense, the men of Sodom were inhospitable to Lot's guests. Apparently, it did not occur to Boswell that possibilities (2) and (4) seem to be at odds. If "to know" the angel's means merely to interrogate them, then, there is no attempted rape only an attempted interrogation. If on the other hand, the men meant to have sexual relations with the visitors (the traditional view) and are guilty of attempted rape, then the interrogation explanation must be abandoned (rendering Boswell's above summary of the views of modern scholarship somewhat incoherent). Some of these explanations, however, are not mutually exclusive and may have been factors in their own way. For example, the general wickedness of Sodom and Gomorrah (1) could have included rape (2) and/or inhospitality (4). My principle concern here is to determine if the biblical record indicates that (4) homosexuality factored in at all. Why did God destroy Sodom and Gomorrah? We can find clues not just from the Genesis account, but also from the Prophets and the New Testament books 2 Peter and Jude. These give a sense of how ancient Jewish thinkers steeped in Jewish culture understood these texts.

First, Sodom and Gomorrah were judged because of grave sin. Genesis 18:20 says, "And the Lord said, 'The outcry of Sodom and Gomorrah is indeed great, and their sin is exceedingly grave.'" Indeed, not even ten righteous people could be found in the city. Second, it seems the judgment of these cities was to serve as a lesson to Abraham and to others that wickedness would be punished. In 2 Peter 2:6 we learn that God condemned and destroyed the cities as "an example to those who would live ungodly thereafter. "Third, peculiar qualities of the sin are described by Jude and Peter. Jude 7 depicts the activity as "gross immorality" and going after "strange flesh." Peter wrote that Lot was "oppressed by the sensual conduct of unprincipled men," and "by what he saw and heard...felt his righteous soul tormented day after day with their lawless deeds." These people were "those who indulged the flesh in its corrupt desires and despised authority" (2 Peter 2:7-10). Piecing together the biblical evidence gives us a picture of Sodom's offense. The sin of Sodom and Gomorrah was some kind of activity—a grave, ongoing, lawless, sensuous activity—that Lot saw and heard and that tormented him as he witnessed it day after day. It was an activity in which the inhabitants indulged the flesh in corrupt desires by going after strange flesh, ultimately bringing upon them the most extensive judgment anywhere in the Bible outside of the book of Revelation. Was the city destroyed because the men of Sodom tried to rape the angels (option (2) above)? The answer is obviously no. God's judgment could not have been for the rapacious attempt itself because His decision to destroy the cities was made days <u>before</u> the encounter (see Genesis 18:20). Further, Peter makes it clear that the wicked activity was ongoing ("day after day"), not a one-time incident. The outcry had already been going up to God for some time.

## Sodom and Gomorrah

Was this a mere interrogation? Though the Hebrew word *yada* ("to know") has a variety of nuances, it is properly translated in the NASB as "have [sexual] relations with." Though the word does not always have sexual connotations, it frequently does, and this translation is most consistent with the context of Genesis 9:5. There is no evidence that what the townsmen had in mind was a harmless interview. Lot's response—"Please, my brothers, do not act wickedly"—makes it clear they had other intentions. In addition, the same verb is used in the immediate context to describe the daughters who had not "known" a man and who were offered to the mob instead. Are we to understand Lot to be saying, "Please don't question my guests. Here, talk to my daughters, instead. They've never been interviewed"? Did God judge Sodom and Gomorrah for inhospitality? Is it true that God's judgment was not for homosexuality per se, but because the people of the town were discourteous to the visitors, violating sacred sanctuary customs by attempting to rape them? A couple of observations raise serious doubt. First, the suggestion itself is an odd one. To say that the men of Sodom were inhospitable because of the attempted rape is much like saying a husband who's just beaten his wife is an insensitive spouse. It may be true, but it's hardly a meaningful observation given the greater crime. Second—and more to the textual evidence—it doesn't fit the collective biblical description of the conduct that earned God's wrath: a corrupt, lawless, sensuous activity that Lot saw and heard day after day, in which the men went after strange flesh. Third, are we to believe that God annihilated two whole cities because they had bad manners, even granting that such manners were much more important than now? There's no textual evidence that inhospitality was a capital crime. However, homosexuality was punishable by death in Israel (Leviticus 18:22, 20:13).

Does God ignore the capital crime, yet level two entire cities for a wrong that is not listed anywhere as a serious offense? The prevailing modern view of the sin of Sodom and Gomorrah is that the attempted rape of Lot's visitors violated the Mid-East's high code of hospitality (19:9). This inhospitality, however, is an inference, not a specific point made in the text itself. Further, the inhospitality charge is dependent upon—and eclipsed by—the greater crime of rape, yet neither could be the sin of Sodom and Gomorrah because God planned to judge the cities long before either had been committed. What possibility is left? Only one. We know the men of Sodom and Gomorrah were homosexual, "both young and old, all the people from every quarter" (19:4), to the point of disregarding available women (19:5-8). After they were struck sightless they still persisted (19:11). These men were totally given over to an overwhelming passion that did not abate even when they were supernaturally blinded by angels. Homosexuality fits the biblical details. It was the sin that epitomized the gross wickedness of Sodom and Gomorrah—the "grave," "ungodly," "lawless," "sensual conduct of unprincipled men" that tormented Lot as he "saw and heard" it "day after day," the "corrupt desire" of those that went after "strange flesh." In their defense, some will cite Ezekiel 16:49-50: "Behold, this was the guilt of your sister Sodom: she and her daughters had arrogance, abundant food, and careless ease, but she did not help the poor and needy. Thus they were haughty and committed abominations before Me. Therefore I removed them when I saw it." No mention of homosexuality here. Clearly, the general wickedness of Sodom and Gomorrah was great. That's not in question. Our concern here is whether homosexuality was part of that wickedness.

## Sodom and Gomorrah

Our analysis of Genesis shows that homosexuality was the principle behavior at issue in that passage. Ezekiel simply enumerates additional sins. The prophet doesn't contradict Moses, but rather gives more detail. Stinginess and arrogance alone did not draw God's wrath. Ezekiel anchored the list of crimes with the word "abominations." This word takes us right back to homosexuality. The conduct Moses refers to in Genesis 18 he later describes in Leviticus as "abomination" in God's eyes. But as for you [the "sons of Israel" (v. 2)], you are to keep My statutes and My judgments, and shall not do any of these abominations, neither the native, nor the alien who sojourns among you for the men of the land who have been before you have done all these abominations, and the land has become defiled. (18:26-27) Moses spoke as clearly here as he did in Genesis. The cities of Sodom and Gomorrah were guilty of many things, but foremost among them was the sin of homosexuality. In this section of Leviticus, God gives directives not just for ritual purity, but commands to be observed by every Jew, <u>and even by every visitor</u>. Homosexuality was wrong for the Jews. It was wrong for gentiles who visited the Jews ("aliens"). It was even an abomination that defiled the land when practiced by pagans who inhabited Canaan long before the Jews came. Homosexuality is a defiling sin, regardless who practices it. It has no place before God among any people, in any age, then or now. One of the more common arguments against homosexuality used to be the destruction of Sodom and Gomorrah. We say "used to be," because many biblical scholars and teachers today realize that there is insufficient scriptural backing for that argument. Let us together take a clear, honest look at these cities, and let us determine who the inhabitants were, and why God destroyed them.

## Save The Family

The first thing to realize is that it wasn't just two cities involved. Today, we only remember the names of two, but in truth, God was about to destroy all the cities of the plain. In addition to Sodom and Gomorrah, the cities of Admah, Zeboiim and Zoar were also about to be destroyed. (Gen. 14:2; Deut. 29:23) Zoar was spared so that Lot and his daughters could flee there, but Admah and Zeboiim met the same fate as Sodom and Gomorrah. Another interesting point is that, at least in reference to Sodom and Gomorrah, the Bible doesn't tell us their real names. Consider: The Hebrew word for Sodom is סדם *S'dom* and means "burnt." The Hebrew word for Gomorrah is ' עמורה *Amorah*, and means "a ruined heap." There can be no question that these names were given to the cities after they were destroyed, and were not their original names. The inhabitants of these cities, like all the Canaanites, were worshippers of false gods. These included the god Molech, arguably the most horrible of all the idols of Canaan. Molech was a huge statue with his arms held out in front of him. A fire would be kindled between his arms, and then newborn children would be placed in his arms and burned alive. This was known as "passing your children through the fire to Molech." Other practices engaged in by the Canaanites included adult human sacrifice, cannibalism, and temple prostitution. (Having sexual relations with temple prostitutes as a form of worship in fertility cults.) Is it any wonder that God was determined to destroy these cities? From a spiritual perspective, people who worship idols and engage in the above-mentioned practices are extremely likely to become demon-possessed, and it is quite probable that many, if not most, of the inhabitants of the cities of the plain were possessed. Lot, Abraham's nephew, moved to the city of Sodom with his wife and two daughters. God sent two angels to Sodom in the evening, ostensibly to investigate the rumors of the sinfulness of the city.

## Sodom and Gomorrah

The real purpose of their visit, though, (since God already knew what was going on) was to rescue Lot and his family from the impending destruction. The account of their visit to the city is found in Genesis 19. Lot was sitting in the gate. This is significant. The person, who sat in the gate, that is, the gatekeeper, was entrusted by the rulers of the city to monitor all traffic in and out of the city, and not to admit anyone who could endanger the city in any way. This was a serious responsibility, and the fact that it was given to Lot, who was not a native of the city, but a relative newcomer, was unusual. A word about the angels: Forget, for a moment, the traditional stereotypes of angels, that is, women with flowing blond hair and huge feathered wings. In scripture, angels usually appeared in the form of men. Frequently, there was nothing unusual about their appearance that would suggest they were anything other than human beings. Lot greeted the two visitors, as was his responsibility as gatekeeper. (He bowed to the ground, which was not an uncommon form of greeting from an inferior to a superior, in this case, from a public servant to strangers whose social status was unknown.) He then evidently inquired about their business in the city and specific destination, again, as part of his job. Upon learning that they intended to spend the night in the street, Lot insisted that they stay at his house. Some have argued that this was because he knew they would not be safe in the streets. The obvious aside, that there has probably never been a city where it is safe to sleep in the streets at night, the reason for Lot's insistence was actually quite different. It was simply the law of hospitality. This law was unwritten at the time, but was universal throughout the area. It simply stated that if a stranger came to your home or city, you were to treat them as if they were part of your family. You were responsible to lodge, feed and protect them, even at the cost of your own life.

## Save The Family

Examples of Abraham treating strangers in this way can be found both in scripture and other Jewish writings. This law was later included in the Law of Moses. After much urging from Lot, the two visitors went to Lot's house and he made dinner for them. Later that night, a mob formed outside of Lot's house, demanding he bring out the guests. Traditionalists would have us believe that the mob was made up of homosexual men, wanting to have sex with the angels. But a careful reading of the verses shows clearly that this was not the case. Gen. 19:4 tells us "*But before they lay down, the men of the city, even the men of Sodom, compassed the house round, both old and young, all the people from every quarter.*" At first glance, it does appear to be a crowd of men. But let's look deeper. The phrase "*the men of the city, even the men of Sodom*" is a bit misleading. In Hebrew, "אנשי העיר אנשי סדם *anshei ha'ir, anshei S'dom,*" could also be translated as *"the people of the city, the people of Sodom."* But is that a more correct translation? The rest of the verse will answer that for us: "...both old and young, **all the people** from every quarter." There is no question, then, that the entire population of Sodom gathered outside Lot's house, men, women and children. This alone tells us that the traditionalists were wrong about the intent of this mob: If you are planning a homosexual orgy, you don't invite the wife and kids! Of course, this begs the question, how did this mob come to form, and what did they want? The Bible doesn't tell us, so we have to read between the lines and in so doing, backtrack from the mob scene outside Lot's house to where the crowd first gathered. First, the fact that the entire population of the city was involved tells us that this was, to them, a matter of vital civic importance. They evidently felt that the visit of these two strangers was something that could affect every person in the city in some way.

## Sodom and Gomorrah

So logic suggests that the gathering would have begun at whatever public place Sodom used for such things, such as a City Hall or public square. Here was the situation as they would have seen it: Lot, a stranger who moved here and was given a position of some responsibility, has invited two strangers of unknown origin into the city and into his home. Sodom had only recently come out of war (Gen. 14:1-2), and for all they knew, these men could have been spies. It was essential for the safety and peace of mind of all the citizens, that they determine the identity of these men. They knew, of course, of the law of hospitality, but the safety and security of the city overrode that. So a plan was devised: They would peacefully go to Lot's house and ask to meet the strangers and know who they were. They even had their words chosen: "Where are the men who came to you tonight? Bring them out and let us know them." It should be noted that this was phrased as a request, using a polite form of the verb *"to know,"* and was not phrased in a hostile, demanding way. And so the crowd began to move toward Lot's house. Between their starting point and Lot's house, something happened to this crowd of concerned citizens that turned them into a mob. When they reached Lot's house, they delivered their prepared request, but even though the grammar was still very polite, the character of the people was now that of an ugly lynch mob. What could have happened? If the people of Sodom were possessed, as they most likely were, this would explain what happened. Even though the people did not know the visitors were angels, the evil spirits inside of them did. When you put a devil in the presence of someone holy, there will almost always be a reaction from the devil. (See Mark 5:1-7) The closer this crowd got to the angels at Lot's house, the more riled up the demons got, and the more out of control the people got.

This seems the only plausible explanation. The polite grammar of the crowd shows clearly that they could not have started out as a mob. There are those who claim that when the crowd said *"let us know them,"* they meant *"have sex."* There are even translations of the Bible that say *"let us have sex with them,"* or *"let us know them carnally."* Let us state categorically, that the Hebrew text will NOT support such "translations." Some say that Hebrew has more than one verb for *"know"* and that the one used here means *"have sex."* Let's set the record straight on this. The root of the Hebrew verb for *"know"* is ידע/*yada*. A form of *yada* is used here and hundreds of other times in scripture. Only about ten of those times refer to sex, and in each case, the sexual meaning is clear by the context. (Example: Adam knew his wife and she conceived.) To try to make this word mean sex everywhere will get us in a lot of trouble, because the scripture tells us that God knew David, and uses a form of this word. We don't think anyone would be foolish enough to try to attach a sexual meaning to that. When the crowd outside Lot's house said they wanted to know the visitors, they meant exactly that: To know who they were. Or at least, that was what they meant when they started out.

*Then the Lord said, "Because the outcry against Sodom and Gomorrah is great and their sin is very grave, I will go down to see whether they have done altogether according to the outcry which has come to me; and if not, I will know... The two angels came to Sodom in the evening; and Lot was sitting in the gate of Sodom. When Lot saw them, he rose to meet them, and bowed himself with his face to the earth, and said, "My lords, turn aside, I pray you, to your servant's house and spend the night, and wash your feet; then you may rise up early and go on your way."*

## Sodom and Gomorrah

*They said, "No; we will spend the night in the street." But he urged them strongly; so they turned aside to him and entered his house; and he made them a feast, and baked unleavened bread, and they ate. But before they lay down, the men of the city, the men of Sodom, both young and old, all the people to the last man, surrounded the house; and they called to Lot, "Where are the men who came to you tonight? Bring them out to us, that we may know them."* To understand scripture, you've got to look at the whole picture - in context - which means you've got to understand what people were doing at the time and what was going on in the culture: spiritually, historically and physically. You've got to let scripture explain itself; you've got to look at what words meant when they were originally written, not how we interpret them today. Words often change meanings from one generation to another, even from one group to another. Just ask a British-speaking individual. You've got to the let the Holy Spirit guide your interpretation and your understanding. And -- most important -- you must understand the very simple basic meaning of the whole body of scripture, which is to love God and to love and care for each other. What is not in agreement with this essential truth is against God. Jesus Himself did not always follow the laws: in every case, He chose the humane route rather than the legal, the way of love and not the way of law. For generations people have blamed the destruction of Sodom and Gomorrah on homosexuality. Was it or was homosexuality a convenient excuse? What was the real reason Sodom was destroyed? We need to understand the cultural, historical, physical and spiritual context before we can hope to understand the meaning of this scripture. 1) Who were the Sodomites?

What is the meaning of the term "sodomite" According to Unger's Bible Dictionary, the people of the area worshipped fertility gods, chief among them were Baal/Ashtoreth (Astarte, Asherah - she had many names). This was the female goddess of war and fertility, sensual love and maternity. "She and her colleagues specialized in sex and war and her shrines were temples of legalized vice". Her worship practices were basically orgies, with worshippers *required* to have sex with the priests and priestesses. The priests or male prostitutes, *according to Unger*, who were consecrated to her cult "were styled *qedishim*, 'sodomites' (Deuteronomy 23:18; 1 Kings 14:24; 15:12; 22:46). Here is how Unger describes "sodomite" based on scriptural references (p. 1035): "**Sodomite** (Heb. *qadesh, consecrated, devoted*). The sodomites were not inhabitants of Sodom, nor their descendents, but men *consecrated* to the unnatural vice of Sodom (Gen. 19:5; compare with Romans 1:27) as a religious rite. This dreadful 'consecration,' or, rather, desecration, was spread in different forms over Phoenicia, Syria, Phrygia, Assyria, and Babylonia. Ashtaroth, the Greek Astarte, was its chief object. The term was especially applied to the emasculated priests of Cybele, called Galli, perhaps from the river Gallus in Bithynia, which was said to make those who drank it mad."

## Sodom and Gomorrah

Spiritually, the people of the plains (as the people of Sodom, Gomorrah, and three other area cities) were called, followed fertility gods and goddesses whose practices relied on sexuality as a magical means of ensuring fertile crops and fertile wombs. The eunuch priests of the Great Mother Goddess (called Aruru, Astarte, Ishtar, and other names, depending on the location) engaged in sex with male worshippers who wanted to earn the goddess' blessings. Robert Graves described these priests as the "dog priests" or "Enariae," whose high holiday fell on the Dog days at the rising of the Dog-star, Sirius. It is from these worship practices that scholars believe the ancient Hebrews drew the derogatory term, "dog," to describe these priests. But more on this later. The Great Goddess or Great Mother was the one who granted fertility to humans, animals and crops, according to the people in the land. By worshipping the Great Mother, by any of her names, one could be guaranteed fertility. The worship involved what is called sympathetic magic, i.e., "...to make the corn grow high, one leaps into the air; in order to kill one's enemy, one sticks pins into his effigy" So, to ensure rebirth of crops, you cast your seed (sperm) into the representatives of the Great Mother, her priests or priestesses. The males were even better than the females, since "they had made a greater sacrifice: they had offered to the goddess their manhood" So, basically, these people were engaging in licentious sexual practices as a way of worship and prostituting themselves. 2) What was the great outcry, which had come to the Lord, causing God to come down to earth to check personally? According to George Edwards in <u>Gay/Lesbian Liberation: A Biblical Perspective</u>, the word "outcry" comes from the word *zecaqa*, "a technical legal term... signifying 'the cry for help which one who suffers great injustice screams.'"

It is the cry of the poor and homeless, of the innocent and powerless for justice. In Sodom, the Hebrews perceived a people whose disdain for the rights of others characterized the entire Canaanite people. Scripture explains the sins of Sodom over and over. In no case is it homosexuality. In all cases, Sodom's doom is caused by its inhospitality. In every case, scripture demands that the rights of the alien and dispossessed be upheld. **The answer is in Ezekiel 16:49-50. This is what Sodom did wrong.** *Behold, this was the guilt of your sister Sodom: she and her daughters had pride, surfeit of food, and prosperous ease, but did not aid the poor and needy. They were haughty, and did abominable things before me; therefore I removed them, when I saw it.* Aha, "abominable things" must surely refer to homosexuality, they say, totally ignoring what is said about pride and compassion.

According to this information:

"This word [abomination] is used to denote that which is particularly offensive to the moral sense, the religious feeling, or the natural inclination of the soul....The practices of sin -- such as the swelling of pride, lips of falsehood, the sacrifices of the wicked, and the foul rites of idolatry -- are stigmatized as abominations... "Remember Ashteroth? Homosexuality? 3) "...that we may know them." The Hebrew word used here is *yadha*, meaning "know. "According to F. Brown, S.R. Driver and C.A. Briggs, *A Hebrew and English Lexicon of the Old Testament* (Oxford, 1952), the verb *yadha* occurs 943 times in the Old Testament. Derrick S. Bailey, in *Homosexuality and the Western Christian Tradition* (Archon Books, 1975), says that the verb is used only ten times as a reference to sexual "knowing." Further, he says (pages 2-3): "In combination with *mishkabh*, which signifies in this context the act of lying, *yadha* occurs in five further places.

## Sodom and Gomorrah

On the other hand, *shakhabh* (from which *mishkabh* comes) is found some fifty times meaning 'lie' in the coital sense. Moreover, while *yadha* always refers to heterosexual coitus (omitting from consideration for the present the disputed passages, Genesis 19:5 and Judges 19:22), *shakhabh* is used of both homosexual and bestial coitus, in addition to that between man and woman. "Does the word here mean "to have homosexual sex" with the angels? Or does it mean to know who these strangers are who have come to stay with the other outsider, Lot? 4) Lack of care for others is a sin mentioned in Ezekiel. And many people refer to the sin of Sodom as lack of hospitality. In that type of climate, hospitality or lack of it meant life or death for travelers. Look at the sharp contrast in the way the angels were greeted by Abraham, *just before they went to Sodom*, and the way they were greeted by the Sodomites. *[Abraham] lifted up his eyes and looked, behold, three men were standing opposite him; and when he saw them, he ran from the tent door to meet them, and bowed himself to the earth, and said, "My lord, if now I have found favor in your sight, please do not pass your servant by. Please let a little water be brought, and wash your feet, and rest yourselves under the tree; and I will bring a piece of bread, that you may refresh yourselves, and after that you may go on.... Abraham also ran to the herd, and took a tender and choice calf... And he took curds, and milk, and the calf which he had prepared, and placed it before them; and he stood by them under the tree as they ate. (Genesis 18:2-8)* (New American Standard) Abraham is considered a righteous man by God, and God's "friend." God could not find *ten* righteous people in Sodom and so destroyed it.

5) Rape To get a better picture of the rape factor in the Sodom story, you also need to compare a story in <u>Judges 19</u>. This story is almost a direct parallel to the Sodom story in many ways. The story goes as follows: a man was travelling with his concubine and stays one night in the city of Gibeah. The man and woman are received by an old man who was a "sojourner" (like Lot was) in the city and are surrounded during the night by the citizens of the town who demand to "know" the man. The old man offers them his daughter and the man's concubine. The visitor sends his concubine out, and she is raped all night by the men of the city, finally dying in the morning on the doorstep. Would homosexual men rape a woman all night because they couldn't get a man?? Hello?? As closely parallel these two stories are, interpreters *never* put the blame on homosexuality, but always on inhospitality.

6) Sex between species

The Scriptures *do* talk about sexual relations between women and angels and that this is so abhorrent to God that God destroyed the world because of it. Look at Genesis 6:2-6: *...the sons of God* [the common way angels are referred to in Scripture] *saw that the daughters of men were beautiful; and they took wives for themselves, whomever they chose. Then the LORD said, "" My Spirit shall not strive with man forever, because he also is flesh... The Nephilim were on the earth in those days, and also afterward, when the sons of God came in to the daughters of men, and they bore children to them. Those were the mighty men who were of old, men of renown. Then the LORD saw that the wickedness of man was great on the earth, and that every intent of the thoughts of his heart was only evil continually. The LORD was sorry that He had made man on the earth, and He was grieved in His heart.*

## Sodom and Gomorrah

(New American Standard). Compare this to Jude 6-7 where Jude talks about angels doing what come unnaturally: *And the angels who did not keep their own position but abandoned their proper abode [God] has kept... in eternal bonds under darkness for the judgment of the great day; just as Sodom and Gomorrah and the cities around them, since they in the same way as these indulged in gross immorality and went after strange flesh, are exhibited as an example, in undergoing the punishment of eternal fire.* (New American Standard) It seems that inter-species relations are forbidden and grieve God as an unnatural thing. Finally, if the Sodom story talks about sexual use, it is in the context of idolatry (worship of false gods), violent rape, interspecies relations. If Sodom was destroyed because of non-sexual reasons, there is also much evidence for it. The story of Sodom tells us as gay Christians to worship God alone, to engage in no sexual practices during worship, to be caring and compassionate toward strangers. Who knows? They might be angels. In closing, this story from Robert Graves' and Raphael Patai's book, *Hebrew Myths* (Greenwich House, 1983), gives a telling clue to the truth behind the Sodom story (pages 167-168): *The Sodomites were among the richest of nations....*

*Sodom was secure against attack; yet to discourage visitors, its citizens passed a law that whoever offered a stranger food should be burned alive. Instead, the stranger must be robbed of all he had and flung from the city stark naked. Once a year they held a feast.... When they had well drunken, every man would seize his neighbor's wife, or his virgin daughter, and enjoy her. Nor did any many care whether his wife or daughter were sporting with his neighbor; but all made merry together from dawn to dusk, during those four days of festival....Beds were placed in the streets of Sodom for measuring strangers.*

## Save The Family

*If a man proved to be shorter than the bed on which he had been laid, three Sodomites would seize his legs, three more his head and arms, and stretch him until he fitted it. But if he proved to be longer than the bed, they forced his head downward and his legs upward. When the poor wretch cried out in a death agony, the Sodomites said, 'Peace, this is an ancient custom here.' In the city of Admah, near Sodom, lived a rich man's daughter. One day a wayfarer sat down by her house door, and she fetched him bread and water. The city judges, hearing of this criminal act, had her stripped naked, smeared with honey, and laid beside a wild bees' nest; the bees then came and stung her to death. It was her cries that prompted God's destruction of Sodom, Gomorrah, Admah and Zeboyim; also those uttered by Lot's elder daughter, Paltit -- who had given a needy old man water, and was dragged to the stake for her obstinate ways.*

"*You shall not lie with a male as one lies with a female; it is an abomination.*" *Leviticus 18:22.* "*If there is a man who lies with a male as those who lie with a woman, both of them have committed a detestable act; they shall surely be put to death....*" *Leviticus 20:13* (New American Standard) The two references in Leviticus are the only direct references to homosexuality in the Old Testament. (And if one were to look at it narrowly, it really only applies to male Jews, sincle only males are addressed, and since Christians consider themselves in a state of grace, not under the law -- or why then do they eat shellfish and pork?) Just as in the case of Sodom and Gomorrah, one must look at the cultural setting in which Letivicus was written, the words used, and the context to truly understand what the Scripture is talking about. Here, as in many other places in both parts of the Scriptures, the cultural and contextual condemnation is of idolatry.

## Sodom and Gomorrah

Passages denouncing other forms of cultic worship surround both Levitical references. John McNeil, in <u>The Church and the Homosexual</u>, writes that any time homosexual activity is mentioned in the Old Testament, "the author usually has in mind the use male worshippers made of male prostitutes provided by temple authorities." Male cult or temple prostitution was enormously popular during all the period of Scripture and seemed to have been awfully attractive to many of the Hebrews, leading to the demand in Deuteronomy 23:17-18: *None of the daughters of Israel shall be a cult prostitute, nor shall any of the sons of Israel be a cult prostitute. You shall not bring the hire of harlot or the wages of a dog into the house of the Lord your God..., for both of these are an abomination to the Lord your God.* Male priests of the Great Goddess were called dogs by the Hebrews. David Greenberg, in <u>The Construction of Homosexuality</u>, finds further support for this in other nearby ancient cultures: among others, a fourth century B.C. Phoenician inscription found on Cyprus "refers to a category of temple personnel who played a role in the sacred service of Astarte, identifies the *kelev* (dog) as a religious functionary.... The Sumerogram [a picture-word] for *assinu*, a male-homosexual cult prostitute... joines the symbols for 'dog' and 'woman.'" Greenberg points out Hittite, Babylonian and Assyrian texts which refer to these male prostitutes. The texts picture *assinu* and *kurgarru* as "religious functionaries particularly associated with the goddess Ishtar, who danced, played musical instruments, wore masks, and were considered effeminate.... such functionaries were believed to have magical powers... 'if a man touches the head of an *assinu*, he will conquer his enemy'... 'if a man has intercourse with an *assinu*, trouble will leave him.'"

Sumerian priests, Greenberg says, held titles which, translated literally, meant "'womb', 'penis-anus,' and 'anus-womb.'... Sumerian preistesses were called *assinutum*.... Babylonian and Assyrian cuneiform texts assert that 'the high priestess will permit intercourse per anum in order to avoid pregnancy.'" Even later, during Roman And Christian rule, the Great Goddess and her eunuch priests attracted many worshippers. Lucian, in *The Syrian Goddess*, described how the Galli, the eunuch priests of the Goddess, would "'...sing and celebrate their orgies... [to become one of the Galli, a young man] strips off his clothes and with a loud shout bursts into the midst of the crowd and picks a sword.... He takes it and castrates himself, and runs wild through the city bearing in his hands what he has cut off. He casts it into any house at will, and from this house he receives women's rament and ornaments.'" On the other hand, your average male worshipper would simply have sex with the male priests to offer his semen to the goddess. The Bishop of Caesarea, Eusebius (260?-340? A.D.) wrote in *The Life of Constantine* that the goddess worshipers still held homosexual cult worship on Mount Lebanon. So, culturally, the Hebrews were surrounded by religious worship which involved the use of male homosexual practices. In context, our references are also surrounded by references to other religious practices. Leviticus 18:21 reads: *Neither shall you give any of your offspring to offer them to Molech....* The verses which follow 18:22 read: *Also you shall not have intercourse with any animal to be defiled with it, nor shall any woman stand before an animal to mate with it.... Do not defile yourselves by any of these things; for by all these the nations which I am casting out before you have become defiled.* Apparently George Edwards, <u>Gay/Lesbian Liberation: A Biblical Perspective</u>, this practice was tied in to an Egyptian ram cult.

## Sodom and Gomorrah

The Bishop of Caesarea, Eusebius (260?-340? A.D.) wrote in *The Life of Constantine* that the goddess worshipers still held homosexual cult worship on Mount Lebanon. So, culturally, the Hebrew were surrounded by religious worship which involved the use of male homosexual practices. In context, our references are also surrounded by references to other religious practices. Leviticus 18:21 reads: *Neither shall you give any of your offspring to offer them to Molech....* The verses which follow 18:22 read: *Also you shall not have intercourse with any animal to be defiled with it, nor shall any woman stand before an animal to mate with it.... Do not defile yourselves by any of these things; for by all these the nations which I am casting out before you have become defiled.* Apparently George Edwards, Gay/Lesbian Liberation: A Biblical Perspective, this practice was tied in to an Egyptian ram cult. Do these laws then apply? There are still people who worship idols, using sexual activity in their worshipping services, and who sacrifice infants to demon gods. To these people I believe the Law still applies. To the people naturally gay or lesbian seeking committed, stable, healthy relationships, I do not believe these laws apply. *For even though they knew God, they did not honor God as God or give thanks, but they became futile in their speculations, and their foolish heart was darkened. Professing to be wise, they became fools, and exchanged the glory of the incorruptible God for an image in the form of corruptible man and of birds and four-footed animals and crawling creatures.* **Therefore** *God gave them over in the lusts of their hearts to impurity, so that their bodies would be dishonored among them.*

*For they exchanged the truth of God for a lie, and worshiped and served the creature rather than the Creator, who is blessed forever. Amen.* ***For this reason*** *God gave them over to degrading passions; for their women exchanged the natural function for that which is unnatural, and in the same way also the men abandoned the natural function of the woman and burned in their desire toward one another, men with men committing indecent acts and receiving in their own persons the due penalty of their error. And just as they did not see fit to acknowledge God any longer, God gave them over to a depraved mind, to do those things which are not proper, being filled with all unrighteousness, wickedness, greed, evil; full of envy, murder, strife, deceit, malice; they are gossips, slanderers, haters of God, insolent, arrogant, boastful, inventors of evil, disobedient to parents, without understanding, untrustworthy, unloving, and unmerciful* **Romans 1:21-21** (The Kingdom Culture English Standard Bible) In context, this passage says that those who know God and do not give God credit, God gives over to all kinds of depravity: they become lustful and unloving and gossips, among other things. But funny thing, only one part of this passage is pulled out. You <u>cannot</u> take one or two verses out of a whole story and interpret them apart from the story. Yet verses 26 and 27 are nearly always used out of context against all gay and lesbian people. Just as when we've looked at the other passages in scripture, we need to really look at what words were used, how the words are used, then at the cultural context (in other words, what activity was Paul trying to address when he wrote this letter). First, in Romans 26, Paul uses the term "para phusin," which means "against nature." It is this phrase that gave its name to the "Crimes Against Nature" laws. But Paul also uses the same phrase in other places.

## Sodom and Gomorrah

For example, in Romans 11:24, where God grafts the gentiles "contrary to nature" onto the Jewish olive tree; Galatians 2:15, where he says Jews are Jews "by nature"; and 1 Corinthians 11:14, where he says that nature teaches that "...if a man has long hair, it is a shame unto him," in spite of the fact that Leviticus says for a man never to cut his hair or round the corners of his beard (Leviticus 19:27). By Paul's use of this phrase, it appears that "nature" to him is "a matter of training and social conditioning," in other words, what is proper according to custom. The reality *is* that "unnatural" usually means something *you* don't want to do, rather than something that is really Unnatural. It's unnatural to shave. It's unnatural to eat popcorn from the microwave. It's unnatural -- isn't it? -- to fly in big metal tanks (I mean, if God wanted us to fly, God would've given us wings.) But it sure would be unnatural to give it up now, wouldn't it? Is it unnatural for a certain number of people in every culture and time to fall in love with members of their own sex? Actually, no. Another of the words used, in Romans 1:27 is the Greek word *katergazomai*. According to Rev. Bob Arthur, former Assistant Dean of Men at Bob Jones University, and Greek and Semitic language scholar, "The work *ergazomai* alone means to work or accomplish. But when the preposition *kat* is put with it, the extreme energy required to accomplish that deed is referred to. "This would indicate a violation of the natural tendencies of that man who has sex with another man. Could the act of rape be indicated by selecting this particular verb? At any rate, for a gay man, whose natural preference is for other men, it would certainly not require *katergazomai* to accomplish a sexual act with another man" ("Homosexuality and the Conservative Christian,").

Other scholars as well have interpreted the passage in Romans 1:26 to refer to people who have consciously *chosen* to have sex in some manner which is not normal for them. (And certainly, there are people who *do* so choose, even today. Most gay or lesbian people have never consciously chosen to be attracted to a member of the same sex.) The use of another Greek word *aphentes*, according to Father McNeill "...strengthens the image of a conscious choice...."Paul in this passage appears to believe that this unnatural homosexual activity was a result of idolatry ("*Therefore* God gave them up..."). God punished the idolator by allowing them the consequences of their own choice, giving up on them, if you will. The whole point of the first chapter of Romans is that God's power and reality are obvious to anyone who looks around and that people must consciously choose to turn from God. God's anger is directed against those who deliberately choose to turn away from worshipping God to worshipping or giving magical power to objects, animals, other people, or even to "self." Things haven't changed. Anything one loves more than God is an idol. Lust is love so misdirected. According to Bob Arthur, Paul talks about three kinds of lust in this chapter. Verse 22 involved the lust for wisdom, which results in foolishness. Verse 26 talks about women's lust for sex, and the natural result is a perversion of natural love into something unnatural for that individual ("Paul does not specify what the unnatural sexual conduct is. For different people it could be different things"). Verse 27 talks about men allowing sex to become god which leads to them abandoning normal sex for *katergazomai*. "Especially for Christian lesbians and gays, "Arthur continues, "This passage should not apply. For to a Christian, God is first in our lives, and all other desires fall into second place.

## Sodom and Gomorrah

Therefore sex is not a god, and we do not fall under the condemnation described in Romans 1". Even to a non-Christian gay or lesbian, who is simply doing what is perfectly normal and natural, "by nature," verses 26 and 27, by themselves do not apply. *Or did you not know that the unrighteous shall not inherit the kingdom of God? Do not be deceived; neither fornicators, nor idolaters, nor adulterers, nor effeminate, nor homosexuals, nor thieves, nor the covetous, nor drunkards, nor revilers, nor swindlers, shall inherit the kingdom of God.*

*1 Corinthians 6:9-10...law is not made for a righteous one, but for those who are lawless and rebellious, for the ungodly and sinners, for the unholy and profane, for those who kill their fathers or mothers, for murderers and immoral men and homosexuals and kidnappers and liars and perjurers, and whatever else is contrary to sound teaching.*

*1 Timothy 1:9-10* The towns of Corinth and Ephesus (where Timothy was bishop), world-class cities of their day, were also the sex capitals of the world. In fact, according to Rev. David Day, in <u>Things They Never Told You In Sunday School: A Primer For The Christian Homosexual</u>, Corinth was so famous for its sexual activities that the name of the city became a way to describe those activities: "'Corinthian girl' ...meant prostitute, 'Corinthian businessman 'meant whoremonger,... 'to play the Corinthian' ...meant to visit a house of prostitution.... 'Corinthian' became a Greek slang term for the sexually loose" Day says, too, that "The same-sex activity that Paul would have encountered during his missionary visits here would have been associated with idolatry, pederasty, or prostitution and sometimes all of the above....

Many young boys were purchased through the slave trade and castrated to preserve their youthful appearance for the pleasure of their masters" Horner says that in Corinth was the temple of Aphrodite Ourania, which had over a thousand prostitutes, and many Greek men continued to visit them after their conversion to Christianity. In Greek society at the time, these were "no stigma attached to a man having sex quite casually with a male prostitute or with any other member of his own sex. And to the nobler type of homosexual love Greek society attached honor and even virtue" (Horner, p. 91-2). In Ephesus, the temple of Artemis is no longer standing, but Horner reports that one of the first structures pointed out to visitors is the door of a house of prostitution. "It is marked by a tremendous erect penis in stone, the sign Priapus the god of sex. When one has actually seen such things, it is much easier to imagine the intimate connection between religion and sex in Paul's day". The Romans had a little stricter view of homosexuality, although they certainly indulged. Like other "vices," homosexuality, because forbidden, was that much more popular, according to The *Satyricon* of Petronius and *The Lives of the Caesars* by Suetonius. Horner reports that a popular Roman board game was one in which virtues and vices were listed along the side of the board. The "naughty" vices were listed in the vulgarest street language and included: fornicators, idolaters, adulterers, effeminate, abusers of themselves with mankind, thieves, covetous, drunkards, ervilers, extortioners. Adolf Deissman, in his *Light from the Ancient East:* believed that Paul was influenced by the list when he wrote the passage in Corinthians. Paul was using a list of commonly known "vices" as an example for his mostly Greek audience.

## Sodom and Gomorrah

Corinth, though a Greek city, was enormously influenced by Roman culture. And Paul always knew and directed his comments at his specific audience. The first term, *pornoi*, means fornication. It is the word from which we get pornography. And in the context, it meant male prostitute to classical Greek writers and to modern Greeks. In the New Testament it referred to "any person who indulged in sexual relations that were considered irregular..." The way words are translated frequently reflect the translator's prejudice rather than the true meaning. John Boswell, writing in Christianity, Social Tolerance and Homosexuality, gives a couple of examples of culturally-provoked mistranslations: "'In Crete it is considered praiseworthy for a young man to have as many [male] lovers as possible'" becomes "'In Crete...for young men to have the greatest number of love affairs.'" And Ovid's "'inpia virgo'" ("'shameless girl'") who seems to have been engaged in homosexual conduct a few lines above ("specifically characterized as 'natural' by Ovid") becomes "'unnatural girl.'" Two other terms Paul used are the terms frequently translated as "homosexual": *malakoi* and *arsenokoitai*. *Malakoi* actually meant something like "soft things." Jesus used it when He asked the people in Matthew 11:8: "But what did you go out to see? A man dressed in *soft* (*malakos*, the singular of *malakoi*) clothing? Behold, those who wear *soft* clothing are in kings' palaces." *Malakoi* in other contexts was used to mean "sick," "weak-willed," "cowardly," "debauched," "wanting in self control." It is "never used in Greek to designate gay people as a group or even in reference to homosexual acts generically..." Gay men in that period were rarely considered effeminate, according to Boswell, unless they acted in an effeminate manner besides engaging in homosexual activity.

Other words were used to refer to effeminacy, but *malakos* was more "associated with masturbation or general moral laxity." Boswell goes on to say: "It is crucial to bear in mind how different attitudes on these subjects were in Hellenistic [Greek] cities during the centuries preceding and following the birth of Christ. Hercules could engage in any number of homosexual liasons without the slightest loss of prestige or any hint of decreased manliness, but the simple act of wearing a woman's garment or performing tasks traditionally reserved to females would be considered irredeemably degrading". The second term, *arsenokoitai*, is a rarely-used, compound Greek word. The first part, "arseno," is the word for male. The second part, "koitai," according to Boswell "is a coarse word...and in this and other compounds corresponds to the vulgar English word 'fucker'". I like Boswell's comparison of this word to the term "lady killer." In context, we know that this term means someone who is a Don Juan, or a "'wolf.'" But how would someone coming from outside of our culture and unfamiliar with our slang know whether this term means a woman murderer, a murderer of women or what? In the same way, we cannot know for sure what *arsenokoitai* really meant. In fact, *arsenokoitai* could even have referred to women who took the active role in sex -- such women were roundly condemned by Christian and pagan writers alike. Through analysis of other compound words and context, Boswell has determined that, in actuality, the word most likely meant male prostitutes. Boswell also researched the hundreds of writers, pagan and early Christian, who mentioned homosexuality. None of them use the word bishop, Eusebius, understood the word to mean "prostitution of men directed toward women rather than other men."

## Sodom and Gomorrah

By the way, "[Male] Homosexual prostitution was not only tolerated but actually taxed by Christian emperors in Eastern cities for nearly two centuries after Christianity had become the state religion." Homosexual prostitution, according to most scholars and ancient texts was rampant throughout that part of the world, both in and out of cultic worship. Boys were kidnapped and sold regularly for use as prostitutes; many were castrated [made into eunuchs] in order to preserve their youthful appearance longer for their masters.) Homosexuality itself was so commonly written about that Paul could have used any number of words if he wanted to condemn homosexuality in general, but he didn't. Huh, what'd He Say? Jesus or Yeshua as His friends probably called Him, loved people. And He was a RADICAL. He talked to WOMEN, ANY women. He even treated them like real human beings. He said it was better for a woman to learn than to do housework. His thing about divorce stemmed from the fact that men could just toss their wives out the door whenever they got tired of them. That was the law. He said that's not acceptable. I really don't think He would have accepted wife-beating, either. Jesus did have something to say about gay people, as much as He *could* say in that very strict culture where there was no gay lifestyle the way we understand it. He said in Matthew 19:12, "For there are some eunuchs, who were so born from their mother's womb, some are made eunuchs by men, and some make themselves eunuchs for the sake of the kingdom of heaven." He begins and ends this very strange statement by saying, "Not everyone can accept this statement…Only those whom God helps….Let anyone who can, accept my statement." Why did He say this about eunuchs?

Who were eunuchs? By current definition, a eunuch is one who has been castrated. But, according to Bob Arthur, that was not the only New Testament period definition. "The Greek word used in Matthew 19 is *eunouchos*, which is a masculine noun referring to men who are in the state of...being unmarried". Many people today believe eunuchs were without sexual desire. However, that is not the case. The *galli*, for example, the men who castrated themselves during the frenzy of goddess worship, were known for homosexual orgies. In the Hebrew culture, any man whose sexual organs were damaged *in any way* was not permitted to be a priest or to come near the altar because that would defile the altar (Lev. 21:21, 23). Anyone who could not or would not reproduce was considered cursed. But I believe that when Jesus talked about those was made eunuchs in heaven; He was not only talking about those who were made physically unable to marry or to reproduce, but also those who were made so hormonally. I believe that even though many, many gay and lesbian people do have children either through social pressure or deliberate choice, which we are somehow made differently from the beginning. (The question remains: when did *you* choose the person to whom you were attracted? There is some medical evidence for the genetic root of homosexuality, but that's a whole 'nother story.) And who did the Holy Spirit deliberately send Philip the apostle to? The Treasurer of Ethiopia, a eunuch (Acts 8:26-27). God promises eunuchs who love and obey God "...in my house and within my walls a memorial ... an everlasting name which will not be cut off" (Isaiah, 56:4-5). But the major point about Yeshua is that He said, Come to me, ALL ye that are weary and I will give you rest." (He didn't say, "except for....") Greenberg and others have pointed out another "puzzling" passage in scripture.

## Sodom and Gomorrah

In Matthew 5:22, Jesus says: *But I say to you that everyone who is angry with his brother shall be guilty before the court; and whoever shall say to his brother 'Raca,' shall be guilty before the supreme court; and whoever shall say, 'You fool,' shall be guilty enough to go into the fiery hell.* The word *raca*, in Hebrew, means *soft*, with "connotations of effeminacy and weakness. By implication the phrase refers to passive effeminate male homosexuals." Similarly, the syllable *raq* is an Akkadian prefix indicating a woman's name or task. The Akkadian symbol is the one used to indicate a woman. Several scholars have even suggested that the word *moros*, which is translated as *fool*, "actually refers to a male homosexual aggressor". Perhaps, just perhaps, Jesus was telling the people to quit condemning homosexuals. It's worth a thought. Jesus said to a man who asked, "What must I do to have eternal life?" "Don't kill, don't commit adultery, and don't steal, don't lie, honor your father and mother, and love your neighbor as yourself!" (Mat. 19:16, 18-19) Jesus said the two most important commandments are "You shall love the Lord your God with all your heart, and with all your soul, and with all your mind, and with all your strength. "The second is this, 'You shall love your neighbor as yourself.' There is no other commandment greater than these." (Mark 12:30-31) Jesus was incredibly gentle with plain old sinners, including sexual sinners. But He yelled at hypocrites and legalists a lot. He offered a woman (not even Jewish, yet, and living with a fifth man, not her husband) His living water (John 4)—salvation. He said, "…anyone who believes in me will have eternal life. For God loved the world so much that God gave Jesus so that anyone who believes in Him shall not perish but have eternal life.

God did not send the Son into the world to condemn it, but to save it. "There is no eternal doom awaiting those who trust God to save them." (The Kingdom Culture Exploratory Study Bible). In doing this series, and in simply being a part of this culture, I've constantly wondered what on earth has caused our society as a whole to regard homosexuals with such violent and irrational hatred. It seems to me that, as with any disease, we need to find the cause before we can find the cure. I really recommend that anyone interested in more detail about the history of the disease of homophobia read a few of the books listed in the back, especially the classics: Boswell and Greenberg. Greenberg writes a really wonderful cross-cultural and historical account of attitudes toward homosexuality.

**The Origins** In classical Greek culture, Aristophanes described "homosexual desire as a 'natural necessity' like heterosexual desire, eating, drinking and laughing. Xenophon expressed the opinion of most Greeks of his day when he commented that homosexuality was a part of 'human nature.'" Plato's discussions of love assume the "ubiquity of homosexual attraction…where heterosexuality appears in some of them as a somewhat inferior preference". The story of Sodom and Gomorrah had no homosexual inference until New Testament times. Old Testament sources list the sins of Sodom as pride, arrogance, lack of care for other human beings (Ezekiel 16:49, Jeremiah 23:14). Late New Testament books (2 Peter, Jude), written around 150 C.E. (Common Era, the non-Christian equivalent to A.D.) are the first references we have hinting at homosexuality in the Sodom story. Between 100 B.C.E. (Before the Common Era), when the author of 3 Maccabees (an apocryphal book) described the men of Sodom as "workers of arrogance" and 2 Enoch,

## Sodom and Gomorrah

written by a Hellenistic Jew (i.e., one who was under the influence of Greek culture) before the middle of the first century C.E., a major change occurred in interpretation. 2 Enoch identifies the crime of Sodom as "child corruption." But then, this was also the time when Nero had an 8-year-old boy castrated and married him in an elaborate public ceremony that must have completely disgusted the Jews and most other folks. But how could they condemn this behavior without getting in trouble with the Romans? Josephus, a historian, and Philo, a Jewish theologian from Alexandria, both Hellenistic Jews writing at about the same time, chose the Sodom story to describe in lurid detail what was going on around them, using the same details as did Juvenal and Petronius, who wrote about contemporary Roman culture. It was undoubtedly safer to describe "Sodom" instead of "Rome." One could keep one's head on longer. But the people they wrote for knew who they were *really* talking about. The "wickedness of Sodom" was equal in Jewish eyes to "the lawlessness of the Gentiles," whom the Hellenistic Jews saw everywhere engaged in promiscuous and perverse behavior, both in their personal and religious life. Later writers, however, took Josephus' and Philo's writing literally, forgetting that they were really describing Roman behavior. And so Sodom took on the vices that were well-known and common in Rome and Greece. It became a symbol "for every wickedness which offended the devout Jewish spirit—pride, inhospitality, adultery, forgetfulness of God and ingratitude for his blessings". It was the Hellenistic Jews, of whom Paul was one, who were most exposed to the "vices of the Gentiles," and who, as a result, were most antagonistic to homosexuality.

Philo wrote about the Scriptural laws in terms of the behavior he saw. "…he speaks fearfully of the popularity in his day of pederasty among the pagans. It has invaded the cities like a troupe of disorderly revelers. Nowadays both the active and the passive partner boast of their deeds. The effeminate call-boy openly struts about with his perfume, coiffured hair, white powder and rouge on his face. 'In fact the transformation of the male nature to the female is practiced by them as an art and does not raise a blush.'" He continues by writing about the religious processions in which these people are "honored participants…some are even castrated". Josephus suggests, among other things, that the Greeks attribute to the gods the "'intercourse of males' in order to have an excuse to indulge in their unnatural pleasures (*para phusin*)." [*Para phusin* is the same phrase Paul uses in Romans, which is translated "against nature."] **Biology: Or, lesbians don't count** Disgust at the rampant sexuality and disregard for human dignity around them was only part of the cause of their hostility. The other cause was a commonly held belief that the male seed—the sperm—produced the child that the female womb was simply the field into which the seed was planted and in which it grew. The result of this belief was the glorification of the male and the zero status of women. Philo describes "a man who would knowingly plant his seed in a barren woman [as] an enemy of God and an enemy of nature". This idea of wasting male seed was the source of the Christian tradition equating masturbation and abortion. It was also the reason lesbianism was basically ignored.

## Sodom and Gomorrah

This male glorification at the expense of women in Greco-Roman and Judeo-Christian traditions fed the hatred, because they felt that the male who acted the part of the female in dress or sex act lowered himself to the level of the female and gave up the "glory" of his maleness. This attitude certainly exists today. In classic Greek society, it was fine for a man to be the active sex partner in Greek society. He was honored and considered a "man's man." It was okay for a youth or a slave or a male prostitute to be the passive sex partner, because they had no status anyway. But a man lost status if he dressed or "submitted" himself like a woman. The man who acted this way degraded himself and *all* men. It was *never* okay to have sex with a child. **Changing legal status: A quick run through history** Homosexuality was legal until the third century C.E., when Roman laws began regulating various homosexual activities. Only in the sixth century was it totally prohibited. Between the fourth and sixth centuries, the Roman Empire fell apart. As it was dissolving, Roman society became increasingly intolerant of sexual freedom. Christianity, the only organized political force to survive this period simply adopted and continued this intolerance. Mostly the issue of homosexuality itself was ignored. There were too many survival issues to deal with. A number of early church "fathers," like Augustine, had experienced homosexual feelings in their youth and turned bitterly against it, strongly influencing later Christian thought. Other gay people served among the clergy openly or anonymously. In fact, around the beginning of the 12th century, the concept of a married Catholic clergy was soundly suppressed, partly, some believe, as the result of an internal struggle between gay and heterosexually married clergy.

No laws were specifically written against homosexuality until 533, when Justinian ruled that homosexuality was in the same category as adultery, subject to punishment by death. Mostly these laws were directed against personal enemies or to get money from groups of people they didn't approve of. The only ones known by name who were punished were prominent bishops. From 1050 to 1150 in Europe, a lively gay subculture flourished, producing much gay literature. The political atmosphere changed after this and gays were among several groups at whom hostility was increasingly directed. The verses in Leviticus and Romans suddenly turned useful, and were used to make homosexuality a sin equivalent to murder at the Lateran III Council of 1179. Since this was also happening during the time of the Crusades, much was made of associating homosexual acts with the enemy Muslims (who had no such problem with homosexuality): "Throughout the thirteenth century, wanton and violent sexuality were prominent and regular attributes of Muslim society....Muhammed [was] 'the enemy of nature, popularized the vice of sodomy among his people, who sexually abuse not only both genders but even animals.'" .Commonly "heretics, traitors and sodomites" were mentioned together as if they were one thing. The French word for heretic, "bougre," came to refer to gay men (as in "buggery"). Over a period of 200 years, because of the changing political atmosphere, public opinion of homosexual behavior changed from a minor personal activity, "satirized and celebrated in popular verse, to a dangerous, antisocial, and severely sinful aberration". Early Judeo-Christian writers, like Paul, were people *reacting* to what they saw. They took their own experiences (what they saw happening around them), combined that with the currently accepted biological "science" and above all "GODS WORD" upon that time and came up with the conclusion that homosexuality was sinful and perverted.

## Sodom and Gomorrah

People today—hear me—take what they see, combine it with accepted biological science, and come up with conclusions. If, in your experience, gay people whom are healthy, stable, "normal" people, then it is easier to say, "Well, they are still okay people and maybe we've been taught wrong." If the only gay people many know are the ones seen as promiscuous or "weird" or always desperately unhappy or mass murderers, etc., etc., that is how the world will perceive them. It gets back to educating people (*including the homosexual community*) out of wrong perceptions. And sometimes that can be very, very difficult. But it's worth the assignment GOD gave many of us too do! the infamous cities of homosexual sin. Or is that their sin? Certainly, that is how tradition has passed them on to us – even giving us a name (sodomites) for the unspeakable sin and those who commit it. However, most modern Old Testament scholars agree that that may not indeed be true, and that the point of the story was Sodom's violation of the rather strict and universally acknowledged norms of hospitality – a code of ethics one still finds in Middle Eastern cultures today. This unwritten, but fiercely practiced, code of hospitality was a foundation of civil society in Biblical times. The desert is a harsh environment for travelers, and to deny hospitality to a stranger in such a setting was seen to be the height of cruelty. In the Genesis story of Sodom after welcoming two men (whom the story identifies as angels) into his house, Lot is confronted by all the men in the town, who surround the house and demand, "Where are the men who came to you tonight? Bring them out to us, so that we may know them." There is some debate about the word "to know" here. Most scholars would agree that it has the sexual meaning here – but it is very clear that we are talking about homosexual rape, a violent act of aggression – and clearly something we would all condemn and deem worthy of God's punishment.

And just in case you were not convinced of my characterization of the anti-woman bias before, listen to Lot's proposed solution to this dilemma: "I beg you, my brothers, do not act so wickedly. Look I have two daughters who have not known a man; let me bring them out to you, and do to them as you please; only do nothing to these men, for they have come under the shelter of my roof." (vs. 7-8) That passage alone should cure anyone from wanting to quote this story as one with lasting authority and worthy of emulation! [A similar story in Judges 19 has the host offer the men his own virgin daughter and his guest's concubine - the latter of whom is abused and "wantonly raped." By morning she is dead.] Even by the internal standards of the scriptures themselves, such a condemnation of same gender intimate relationships is not the point of the story. The prophet Ezekiel compares the sins of Jerusalem with those of Sodom, which he says had "pride, excess of food, and prosperous ease, but did not aid the poor and needy." (Ezekiel 16:49) No mention of homosexuality being the problem here. The towns of Sodom and Gomorrah, which were an ancient version of wealthy, gated communities, had canceled the law of hospitality to keep strangers from visiting, seeing their wealth, and potentially returning to plunder that wealth. This was the point even Ezekiel drew from the story. Indeed, Jesus' only reference to the notorious town indicates that he also understood that Sodom's infamy came from its inhospitality. Jesus instructs his disciples that if they go into a town and they are not welcomed, to shake the dust from their feet and go on to another, knowing "on that day, it will be more tolerable for Sodom than for that town." (Luke 10:10-13) No mention of homosexuality here, even by Jesus. Sodom's sin is one of inhospitality and injustice.

## Sodom and Gomorrah

Whatever else one makes of this story, it cannot be used to decry loving, committed, lifelong-intentioned monogamous relationships between two people of the same gender. It is simply not about that kind of relationship. The story is about homosexual rape – and like any rape, it is an act of violence, not an act of sexuality. In short, the story of Sodom and Gomorrah, and all references to it elsewhere in scripture, provide no guidance for modern day believers about the morality or immorality of same gender loving people. It simply does not offer an answer to the questions we are asking.

# CHAPTER VII

## The Worlds Way

Throughout civilization, humanity has longed for a better world. Undeniably, nurturing visions of utopia appear to be a powerful, instinctive desire within us. We are all in search of a better place, a world where there is unity and harmony. Humans seek a completely new order of things; one might even call it an intrinsic yearning for a "new world order." You've probably sensed this desire in your own heart. Even during the best of times, we often find ourselves with a vague feeling of discontent. And in times of distress, these longings can become truly overwhelming. Think about when all your best efforts to improve your life seem stymied by forces or events out of your control; or when an unwelcome tragedy comes and a precious loved one dies an untimely death. Or how about when you read the morning paper and the headlines shriek with fresh reports of violence, outbreaks of disease, and millions starving. As you lock your door against the crime in the streets, do you ever wonder if life will always be like this? Or as you stand by a graveside, do you ever long for a new dawn when that person so dear to you could be alive and happy again? In the Bible, you soon find the varied accounts of the power-hungry trying to conquer the planet and establish a new world order. Genesis chapter 10 addresses the earth's first monarch, the mighty Nimrod, who founded the city of Babel (later known as Babylon). He had visions of a new and powerful centralized government, and he built himself a lofty tower to consolidate that vain and dangerous vision. But Nimrod's plans were permanently frustrated when his tower's construction was halted by that well-known universal breakdown in communications.

Nebuchadnezzar, whose life is chronicled in the book of Daniel, came on the scene years later. He brought Babylon to the height of its glory and envisioned extending its influence and power throughout the known world. But you probably already know that Nebuchadnezzar's dreams were interrupted by a seven-year bout of insanity. Then came the Mede and Persian armies led by Cyrus, who also sought a new, glorious government not yet achieved by mankind. But a few centuries down the line, Alexander the Great ended these misbegotten aspirations of the Persians. After conquering them, he rapidly subjugated huge territories for Greece. It has been said that his utopian vision included the search for the fabled "Fountain of Youth," where he hoped his achievements would be rewarded by immortality. But he died tragically young, having never found what did not exist. Alexander's expansive empire was soon divided and conquered by the Romans. Their Caesars then began implementing their unique version of utopia called "Pax Romana"—or Roman Peace. But gradually, history tells that the Roman Empire also crumbled in strife and turmoil. Throughout civilization, humanity has longed for a better world. Undeniably, nurturing visions of utopia appear to be a powerful, instinctive desire within us. We are all in search of a better place, a world where there is unity and harmony. Humans seek a completely new order of things; one might even call it an intrinsic yearning for a "new world order." You've probably sensed this desire in your own heart. Even during the best of times, we often find ourselves with a vague feeling of discontent. And in times of distress, these longings can become truly overwhelming. Think about when all your best efforts to improve your life seem stymied by forces or events out of your control; or when an unwelcome tragedy comes and a precious loved one dies an untimely death.

## The Worlds Way

Or how about when you read the morning paper and the headlines shriek with fresh reports of violence, outbreaks of disease, and millions starving. As you lock your door against the crime in the streets, do you ever wonder if life will always be like this? Or as you stand by a graveside, do you ever long for a new dawn when that person so dear to you could be alive and happy again? In the Bible, you soon find the varied accounts of the power-hungry trying to conquer the planet and establish a new world order. Genesis chapter 10 addresses the earth's first monarch, the mighty Nimrod, who founded the city of Babel (later known as Babylon). He had visions of a new and powerful centralized government, and he built himself a lofty tower to consolidate that vain and dangerous vision. But Nimrod's plans were permanently frustrated when his tower's construction was halted by that well-known universal breakdown in communications. Nebuchadnezzar, whose life is chronicled in the book of Daniel, came on the scene years later. He brought Babylon to the height of its glory and envisioned extending its influence and power throughout the known world. But you probably already know that Nebuchadnezzar's dreams were interrupted by a seven-year bout of insanity. Then came the Mede and Persian armies led by Cyrus, who also sought a new, glorious government not yet achieved by mankind. But a few centuries down the line, Alexander the Great ended these misbegotten aspirations of the Persians. After conquering them, he rapidly subjugated huge territories for Greece. It has been said that his utopian vision included the search for the fabled "Fountain of Youth," where he hoped his achievements would be rewarded by immortality. But he died tragically young, having never found what did not exist. Alexander's expansive empire was soon divided and conquered by the Romans.

Their Caesars then began implementing their unique version of utopia called "Pax Romana"—or Roman Peace. But gradually, history tells that the Roman Empire also crumbled in strife and turmoil. The list of men searching for the elusive all-controlling, one-world government goes on: Charlemagne, Napoleon, Kaiser Wilhelm, and, of course, Stalin, Hitler, and Mao. All of these famous (and infamous) men watched coldly as their grand schemes failed. And even the League of Nations, United Nations, and European Economic Community have all done their part in attempting to establish their own modified versions of the new world order. But we see how even these peacetime organizations fail miserably at bringing people together! So is this chaos of government building and toppling on earth some kind of cosmic joke? Will there never be peace, freedom, and equal opportunity for all? Or are we simply playing a bit role in an enormous planetary game going nowhere? Are all of mankind's best efforts at peace doomed to abject failure? Should we stop looking for the bright dawn of a new morning—a golden age of love and harmony—and get on with real life? Fortunately, the answer is we shouldn't stop searching. And we need not look far for the best resource to find this perfect place of peace—and see why humanity won't get there on its own. Indeed, the Bible has the answers to these deep, heartfelt questions. And ironically, the Bible uses history's greatest failure of a global power grab to make an unforgettable point. Of all the world leaders mentioned previously, none came closer to realizing a golden, united world empire than Nebuchadnezzar. God came in a dream to this great Babylonian king, giving him an amazing vision of the future. You can read all about this episode in Daniel 2. Briefly: While on his bed, Nebuchadnezzar dreamed about a giant mineral statue with a head of gold, breast of silver, a midsection of brass, legs of iron, and feet of iron mixed with clay.

# The Worlds Way

God then provided Nebuchadnezzar the meaning of the unique dream through His exceptional prophet Daniel. The Lord revealed to Daniel, who prayed under the threat of death, the meaning of this imposing image that the king's own soothsayers couldn't unravel. It was shown to Nebuchadnezzar, and to all of us who long to know what the future holds, that the image represented a succession of major kingdoms ruled by man that would ultimately fail— and then culminate with the peaceful kingdom of God. Nebuchadnezzar witnessed that his mighty golden kingdom of Babylon would fall, only to be followed by three successive empires doomed to failure. The last would disintegrate into many separate nations. Daniel foretold that these smaller, separate nations would vainly attempt to reunite through intermarriage, military conquests, and negotiations. They would never succeed. And that's exactly what happened. Babylon, the head of gold, fell as predicted. And it was followed, exactly as foretold, by the kingdoms of Medo-Persia (silver), Greece (brass), and Rome (iron). These were the major empires that ruled the territory inhabited by God's people. Subsequent to the fall But all this doom and gloom has a purpose. At the end of the vision, God reveals "the rest of the story." Humanity's state of existence doesn't end in a state of confusion, always to be frustrated in futile attempts for utopia. In fact, it "ends" with a grand, glorious, and revolutionary transformation—a rebirth if you will. In Nebuchadnezzar's dream, a gigantic heavenly stone breaks into the scene, striking the image on its feet. Then suddenly, the statue completely and violently dissolves into dust. The entire human system of government and religion on earth is brought to a quick and cataclysmic end. Then God Himself takes the stage. But these sometimes frightening words are really a harbinger of hope to those of us searching today.

"And in the days of these kings shall the God of heaven set up a kingdom, which shall never be destroyed: and the kingdom shall not be left to other people, but it shall break in pieces and consume all these kingdoms, and it shall stand for ever" (Daniel 2:44). This great event, when Jesus comes to establish His kingdom on earth, is known as "the blessed hope." Titus 2:11–13 says, "For the grace of God that brings salvation hath appeared to all men, Teaching us that, denying ungodliness and worldly lusts, we should live soberly, righteously, and godly, in this present world; Looking for that blessed hope, and the glorious appearing of the great God and our Savior Jesus Christ." Just before His death, Jesus comforted His disciples with these words of promise: "Let not your heart be troubled: ye believe in God, believe also in me. In my Father's house are many mansions: if it were not so, I would have told you. I go to prepare a place for you. And if I go and prepare a place for you, I will come again, and receive you unto myself; that where I am, there ye may be also" (John 14:1–3). The apostle Paul elaborated on Christ's promise with this beautiful description: "For the Lord himself shall descend from heaven with a shout, with the voice of the archangel, and with the trump of God: and the dead in Christ shall rise first: Then we which are alive and remain shall be caught up together with them in the clouds, to meet the Lord in the air: and so shall we ever be with the Lord" (1 Thessalonians 4:16–17). He goes on to say, "Wherefore comfort one another with these words" (v. 18). And isn't it true? Don't these words bring real comfort to your heart—a thrill to your soul to think that Jesus is, at this very moment, preparing a beautiful home for you in a place where peace, love, harmony, and unity really exist? History shows that mankind cannot manufacture this kind of place.

## The Worlds Way

All of its best efforts have always ended in defeat and disappointment. It's a proven point that all the greatest political, military, economic, and spiritual leaders have not and never will be successful in forging utopia. But God will be successful so now that we know it's just a matter of time, what exactly will this heavenly home be like? Many people picture heaven as a somewhat eerie place where ethereal spirits sit around on clouds, wearing halos, and strumming golden harps. I don't know about you, but frankly, this depiction sounds pretty boring to me! Fortunately, the Bible gives us quite a different picture. Several passages in Scripture provide some fascinating insights into the heaven that's to come. You see, God wants us to know that heaven is a real place; and better, it's more real and more fulfilling than anything we've ever known. The Bible speaks of a beautiful city called the New Jerusalem, which will be God's headquarters. It is described in Revelation 21 and 22. The picture these chapters paint is mind-boggling! First, the city is huge. It stands 375 miles on each side! (If placed on this earth, New Jerusalem would cover most of North Carolina, Virginia, West Virginia, and Maryland, and parts of Ohio, Pennsylvania, and Kentucky!) Second, the city is incredibly beautiful. It has magnificent walls made of solid jasper with 12 foundations, each made from a different type of precious stone, including sapphire, emerald, topaz, and amethyst. And the city's 12 gates are each made of a single pearl! The streets of the city are made of gold so pure that it appears as transparent glass. But we also learn that the streets are not made to simply look at and admire. Zechariah 8:5 says that "the streets of the city shall be full of boys and girls playing." Not only will New Jerusalem be a breathtaking, shimmering sight, it will also be a place to have fun and rejoice. But most awesome, God Himself will dwell among the redeemed within the midst of the city, and a glorious rainbow surrounds His majestic throne (Revelation 4:3).

From beneath His throne, the river of life springs, and on both sides of this river, the tree of life produces a fresh crop of different fruit every month. The walls, foundation, and streets are this beautiful and spectacular, just imagine what your home will be like—the one that Jesus custom-made for you! What an awe-inspiring privilege and reward to have the Chief Architect of the Universe, who knows your heart's desires even better than you do, designing and building your own unique home in this city! But don't you do-it-yourselfers get discouraged. It's clear that you won't just be sitting around in the New Jerusalem, twiddling your thumbs without something to do. You'll have the opportunity to build a country home in the new earth as well. "And they shall build houses, and inhabit them; and they shall plant vineyards, and eat the fruit of them. They shall not build, and another inhabits; they shall not plant, and another eats: for as the days of a tree are the days of my people, and mine elect shall long enjoy the work of their hands" (Isaiah 65:21, 22). An important aspect of this utopian new world order will be the biosphere of heaven: its lifecycle will be eternal, not one cursed with the decay and death of this sin-infected world. The Creation story makes it clear that all of those negative biological processes entered our world as a result of catastrophic sin (Genesis 3:17–19). Thorns will not be around in heaven to pierce your hands, nor will thistles scratch at your feet. Bugs will not bite, and leaves will not die. Sure, it's a little daunting to comprehend how all this will work scientifically—but our minds are limited by what they're familiar with. Heaven will change all that too. Indeed, our brains will certainly never get bored in heaven; you won't miss your TV, and your kids won't remember what a video game means. There will be more to see and do than we ever imagined here on earth, enough to stimulate our minds for eternity.

We'll be able to trace our family tree right back to Noah and Adam. We will be able to personally visit with many of the people we've only read about before (Matthew 8:11). I look forward to talking with Moses and understanding more fully how he played a role in God's great plan! Furthermore, God and His angels will be there to answer many of the questions that have perplexed us here for 6,000 years; we'll probably have questions we didn't even know there were to ask! We will also have an endless list of fascinating things to study. Perhaps Shakespeare said it best when he wrote: "There are more things in heaven and earth ... than are dreamt of in your philosophy." One of the great benefits of this utopian ecosystem will be that animals will not prey upon one another for food. We are told that "The wolf also shall dwell with the lamb, and the leopard shall lie down with the kid; and the calf and the young lion and the fatling together; and a little child shall lead them. And the cow and the bear shall feed; their young ones shall lie down together: and the lion shall eat straw like the ox" (Isaiah 11:6, 7). And further, "The wolf and the lamb shall feed together, and the lion shall eat straw like the bullock: and dust shall be the serpent's meat. They shall not hurt nor destroy in all my holy mountain, says the Lord" (Isaiah 65:25). Obviously, this means quite literally that there'll be pets in heaven. In fact, every animal could potentially be a pet because none of them will be wild; they will not be afraid of us, nor us of them. God does everything perfectly, and in heaven, everyone will find complete love and happiness—including companionship with God's other creatures. People often wonder whether their pets and furry friends from earth will be with them in heaven. Some say this is impossible because animals don't have immortal souls, much less souls. However, this isn't a hindrance at all. Humans don't have immortal souls either; only God has unconditional immortality (1 Timothy 6:13–16).

He will bless His people with immortality as a gift of His grace at the end of the age (2 Timothy 1:10). So if the all-powerful God of the universe wants to surprise and delight us with the gift of resurrected kittens, puppies, horses, fish, rabbits, birds, snakes, turtles, or whatever other critters we love on this earth, He is certainly able to do so! By granting this, in no way would He violate His moral absolutes. We'll just have to wait and see. Human exploration of the cosmos and space travel will know no limits. The Bible declares that Jesus created all the worlds seen and unseen (Hebrews 1:2). And the last time I checked, more than 200 billion suns have been photographed by California's 200-inch telescope. So it would seem plausible that we will find other inhabited worlds, visiting with other created beings! Isaiah 45:18 also says of our world, "He created it not in vain; he formed it to be inhabited." Those other solar systems must be "created not in vain." They light a multitude of worlds. Another scriptural clue is found in Job 1:6. "Now there was a day when the sons of God came to present themselves before the Lord, and Satan came also among them." In Luke 3:38, Adam is called "the son of God." It's quite possible that the "sons of God" in that heavenly council meeting are the first created beings from other planets. Adam should have represented earth, but Satan usurped his birthright. Fortunately, the first Adam's, and subsequently all of humanity's, rights were bought back by the second Adam, Jesus (1 Corinthians 15). We cannot be positively sure that this is what the passage in Job refers to, but many in the Christian world agree this scenario is possible. The Bible also assures us that the righteous loved ones we lost here on earth will be raised to join the living in God's kingdom (Isaiah 26:19; 1 Corinthians 15:51–55; 1 Thessalonians 4:13–18). Being reunited with the redeemed we loved here is undoubtedly one of the things we will enjoy the most.

## The Worlds Way

Imagine just how deeply moved you will be when a baby or child you lost will be brought to you and placed in your arms! And think about looking into the eyes of a parent, spouse, or close friend, who passed away before you, and then embracing their vibrant, glorified bodies and knowing you will never need to part again! Thrilling music is often mentioned in connection with heaven, so you can be sure that playing instruments and singing God's praises will be a big part of our eternal experience. Our Creator is one of immense diversity. I'm sure we'll enjoy an endless variety of delightful music; we won't just be limited to playing harps! The Bible even says that God Himself will sing: "The Lord thy God in the midst of thee is mighty; he will save, he will rejoice over thee with joy; he will rest in his love, he will joy over thee with singing" (Zephaniah 3:17). He also gives many instructions to sing, such as we see in Psalm 100:2. "Serve the Lord with gladness: come before his presence with singing." It would make sense then that the angels who also worship Him would come before Him with singing too. Some find it disconcerting when Jesus says there will be no new marriages in heaven (Matthew 22:30). We shouldn't deny, cover up, or worry over this important concept; He ought to know since heaven is His hometown. First, we must be careful not to assume this passage means that God will hand divorce papers to the redeemed that have harmonious marriages as they first enter the pearly gates. Knowing who God is, that He is the very essence of love, whatever type of relationships we have now will be even more intimate and fulfilling than anything we have experienced here. I think we can trust in Him to plan something wonderful that will not disappoint us. There also might not be any new births, but we know from the Bible that there will be children in heaven. Isaiah 11:6–9 describes heaven and mentions children several times. Malachi 4:2 says that we shall "grow up as calves of the stall."

This seems to indicate that the children of heaven will experience a physical maturing process going on as well as a spiritual one. Of course, we shouldn't forget that no matter how "old" we get in heaven, we will be eternally young. We will never suffer the terrible effects of aging that we must endure on this corrupted earth! Course, the ultimate and culminating experience of heaven will be meeting our Creator God face to face. "Then shall I know even as also I am known" (1 Corinthians 13:12). The book of Revelation comments: "And I heard a great voice out of heaven saying, 'Behold, the tabernacle of God is with men, and he will dwell with them, and they shall be his people, and God himself shall be with them, and be their God. And God shall wipe away all tears from their eyes; and there shall be no more death, neither sorrow, nor crying, neither shall there be any more pain: for the former things are passed away' " (Revelation 21:3, 4). This is the God who created our world, and who created us in His image. He mourned when Satan tempted mankind to fall, and He's also the one who rescued us through Jesus. His unsurpassed love moved Him to implement a perfect plan: to enter into our world, suffer the results of our sin as we do, and then to die for us. And now, as He makes preparations for us to go home, He longs to shine the way and fulfill all of our hopes. God's chosen people waited 4,000 years for the Savior to come the first time. That seemed like a terribly long time, and many lost hope. But He did come. It's a historical fact. And if He came the first time, according to His promise, we have no reason to doubt that He will come again just as He says He will. He isn't like a conqueror of empires who promises glory only to become a tyrannical despot. And He isn't like a politician of today, making countless promises He cannot keep. He is true to His Word. He will do what He says. Always has. You can count on it. Until then, rejoice knowing that we don't have to wait to experience all the benefits we'll have in heaven.

# The Worlds Way

"Peace on earth, good will toward men" is not just a "pie in the sky" that the angels sang about. Knowing what lies ahead, that our future is secure in God's hands, we can have a powerful sense of joy and peace right here and now. Even though we won't see peace among the nations on this earth, we can still have peace in our hearts amidst the chaos. For those who make contact with God in a personal way today, heaven begins now. God becomes the Friend who never forsakes us; the Counselor with all the answers to our questions, and the Partner in all our endeavors. He cleanses us from all sin, and when we ask, He also imparts the power we need to transform our sin-filled lives. That's the kind of heaven we can live in right now. You see, a perfect world would be pure misery for anyone whose heart was not converted—who didn't learn on earth to love what God loves. If you don't turn away from the things that cause Him grief now, what makes you think you will want to please Him in heaven? The Judgment Day will not be a time when God confers a sentence on hapless victims. Ultimately, God always honors our choices; He's not a tyrant. Never has been. In the Old Testament the heathen nations were sometimes called the nations or the Gentiles but they were often called by their separate identities such as Egypt, Assyria, Babylon, Edom, Ammon, Moab, Syria, Tyre etc. In the New Testament there is not nearly as much use of the names of individual nations even of the godless nations but the general term "world" is used. This word world is from the Greek word cosmos that in current English has come to mean the whole universe. Although that was probably one meaning in first century Greek the main meanings in the New Testament are the evil world system including the entertainment, leisure, business, political and military systems of the world, the world in a good sense as mankind and the world in a good sense as the earth the planet or the entire universe.

The Greek word cosmos that is translated world at least in the King James Version of the English Bible means "adornment" and "arrangement". This was a very positive concept with the Greeks and even with many people today. In this web page I will focus on the instances where from the immediate context the word world can best be translated "world system" or in some cases "world system" and "mankind" or perhaps with "the earth". There are also two other words "aeon" and "oikoumene" translated as world in the King James Version of the Bible that are not used as often as the word cosmos that mean respectively an eon or age and the whole inhabited earth from we get our English word ecumenical. The world as the world system with Satan or Lucifer the devil as its god and prince started when Adam and Eve took of the forbidden fruit in the Garden of Eden in disobedience to God's command and at the instigation of the devil through the serpent. Adam did have authority to have dominion over the earth and over all the animals and plants but he forfeited it to Satan represented in the serpent when Adam sinned willfully and took part of the forbidden fruit from the tree of knowledge of good and evil. From that time the world system has been the combination of the actions, thoughts and values of unsaved or straying believers and Satan and evil spirits. These actions, thoughts and values are focused on pleasing self for people and are usually focusing on earthly, fleshly and temporal or this life activities or values or plans as opposed to what God and the Lord Jesus Christ and the Bible encourage of heavenly, spiritual and eternal activities, values or plans. Most governments and other major institutions of all the countries of the world are inclined to the possessions, activities, values and plans of this world system.

## The Worlds Way

The born again Christian is supposed to resist these values and live by Biblical values, activities, words, thoughts and plans instead which are God and Jesus Christ centered and focused on the eternal, spiritual and heavenly rather than self or world or devilish centered. One important trend at this time that is very difficult to ignore is the ongoing process of national or regional systems or institutions or organizations of the world to become increasingly global in nature and influence. As Bible-believing Christians we believe this is a sign of the last days which as that will culminate with a leader or pair of leaders rising up to take control of a one world economic, political, religious and military system. We think these leaders will be the Beast out of the Sea or simply the Beast or the Antichrist that myself and most Bible believing Christians believe will come from the nations and the Beast out of the Land or False Prophet that myself and most Bible believing Christians think will be Jewish. I and other Christians who take the Bible literally including in Bible prophecy think all true or born again Christians will be caught up to heaven before these global dictators are revealed on earth. We believe 7 years of tribulation or unrest and God's judgments will follow in a time characterized by global government especially in the second half of this 7 year tribulation. This will be followed by the world system being taken over from the devil, demons, and ungodly people permanently by God and His Messiah Jesus Christ to rule this world for a thousand years and then a new earth and heavens forever. We think the Tower of Babel in Genesis 10 and 11 was an early attempt at global government that failed because God didn't want to permit it then. The talk of a New World Order and of a New Age will be prominent parts of the last day's one world form of the world system especially as revealed in chapters like Revelation 13 in God's Word the Holy Bible.

The devil took Jesus to a very high mountain and showed Jesus all the kingdoms of the world and the glory of them which means the glory of the political, business, education, military, religious, entertainment, science and technology, sports or other aspects or the world system of all these kingdoms. Some of these things aren't wrong in themselves but they become more unacceptable to God when they are pursued at the expense of God, Jesus Christ, the Holy Spirit, the Bible or the things of heaven, spiritual godly things or eternal things. The devil then offered Jesus all these kingdoms of the world system and their glory if Jesus would fall down and worship him. Although it might sound presumptuous of the devil to offer these things to Jesus the devil was right in saying he had all these things to offer and this is made even clearer in Luke's account in Luke chapter 4. The devil became in control or heir of all these things when he succeeded in getting Adam the first man with whom God originally entrusted dominion over the earth to obey Satan instead of God when Adam willfully took of the forbidden fruit of the tree of knowledge of good and evil in the Garden of Eden. This knowledge of good and evil was later manifest in the different aspects of the world system. However Jesus if he was to be true to His righteous character and especially his earthly mission of demonstrating perfect obedience to the Father's will in life and in death in his first earthly ministry couldn't bow down to a rebel created angel like Satan, the devil or Lucifer. Jesus stated this when he responded to Satan that the scripture says we should only worship the LORD or God the Father although especially after Jesus' death and resurrection God condoned worship of Jesus who was God who became flesh.

# The Worlds Way

The scripture reference in the Gospel of Matthew 4 of Satan offering Jesus the Savior of the world and Redeemer of Israel all the kingdoms of the world (system) if he would worship Satan and Jesus' refusal saying that we should only worship God is as follows: Again, the devil takes him up into an exceeding high mountain, and shows him all the kingdoms of the world, and the glory of them; And said to him, All these things will I give you, if you wilt fall down and worship me. Then said Jesus to him, get from here, Satan: for it is written, you shall worship the Lord your God, and him only shall thou serve. Then the devil leaves him, and, behold, angels came and ministered to him. Gospel of Matthew 4:8-11 this verse states that God's wisdom is different than that of the world system dominated by non-Christian people. God's wisdom is more through humility while the world's way is more through pride and force. The people of the world system in their wisdom did not recognize this but the apostle Paul under divine inspiration says that it is preaching rather than military means that God has chosen to save and bring into a relationship with Him through faith in His Son Jesus Christ and His death for our sins on the cross and resurrection from the dead to give us new life. The scripture reference from 1 Corinthians about the wisdom of the world not being the same as the wisdom of God for the way of salvation is as follows: For after that in the wisdom of God the world by wisdom knew not God, it pleased God by the foolishness of preaching to save them that believe. 1 Corinthians 1:21. This is never popular with people of the world system and not always even with true Christians but is still a basic teaching of God through His Son Jesus Christ. That is that following the Lord Jesus Christ means to take up our cross and deny ourselves of things of the world system that promotes values, materials and experiences neglecting or opposing God, Jesus Christ, Christians and God's Word –

the Holy Bible or the flesh fallen human nature or the devil or demons but that we should instead follow Jesus and seeking for the things of God, heaven, godly spiritual things and eternity. Jesus further says that if we seek to save or preserve our lives after our self or self-interest we will lose them (in eternity) but if we lose our lives of self interest we will find them for eternity and also our life centered on God in this life after we are saved and when we are abiding in Christ or led by His Holy Spirit. Jesus further says in an extreme case what would it profit a man (man or woman) if they gained the whole world (system) with all the aspects of its business, entertainment, science, religion or spirituality, philosophy, education, science and technology, military, sports, arts, political or other systems and lose one's own soul. Or alternatively Jesus asks the reader and asks you and I what shall a man (man or woman) give in exchange for his soul to which the obvious answer is that there is nothing sufficient to give for our soul. Jesus talks about the importance and benefit of denying self and not seeking the things of this world (system) to instead follow Him in that the Son of man (Jesus) will come at His second coming at the end of the tribulation before He sets up the Messianic Kingdom with the glory of his Father and the holy angels to reward every one according to their works. However it should be kept in mind that other scriptures including other words of Jesus make clear that the first and foundational step in our works and self denial is trusting in the Lord Jesus Christ as our Lord and Savior and admitting that we are sinners who can't save ourselves and deserve God's judgment but who can have God's salvation through Jesus and His death on the cross and resurrection as a free gift. The scripture reference from Gospel of Matthew 16 of Jesus' exhortation for His people to deny ourselves and not seek the things of this world system is as follows: said Jesus unto his disciples,

## The Worlds Way

If any man will come after me, let him deny himself, and take up his cross, and follow me. For whosoever will save his life shall lose it: and whosoever will lose his life for my sake will find it. For what is a man profited, if he shall gain the whole world, and lose his own soul? Or what shall a man give in exchange for his soul? For the Son of man shall come in the glory of his Father with his angels; and then he shall reward every man according to his works. Gospel of Matthew 16:24-27. The world system and its component systems such as the business, government, entertainment, media, military, religious systems and the people involved with each hate the Lord Jesus Christ because he testifies of the world system that its works are evil such as encouraging immorality, covetousness, violence, deception, irreverence to God or indifference to God or general selfishness instead of devotion to God and His Son Jesus Christ and the things of eternity, godly spirituality and heaven. Jesus here and other places in the scripture mentions he hates the world because of its works this doesn't even mean that he hates the unsaved or worldly people but that he hates their attachment to this world and the things of time, materiality, self or the flesh or on this world (earth). The world's hatred of Jesus especially the religious aspect of the world was fully manifest when the Jewish religious leaders that wouldn't listen to Jesus and insisted on trying to preserve their influence based on outward morality or ritual rather than a godly heart or in the case of the Saduccees including many of the chief priests due to covetousness and their material wealth, comfort and influence. True believers in the Lord Jesus Christ can also expect to be hated of this world system if we testify of it that its works are evil but this is what God wants as part of our becoming separate from this world and becoming dedicated to him and compelling unsaved people to think of the world system and its shortcomings and the better offer of eternal and abundant life God gives through His Son Jesus Christ.

Jesus in speaking to his brethren according to the flesh, his half brothers through Mary not through Joseph, could say to them the world cannot hate them because at that time they didn't believe in him (John 7:5) and so couldn't see the shortcomings of the world system or rebuke people of the world system for these sins or shortcomings. The scripture reference of the Lord Jesus Christ saying the world hated him because he testified of the world that its works were evil in the Gospel of John 7 is as follows: The world (system) cannot hate you; but me it hates, because I testify of it, that the works thereof are evil. Gospel of John 7:7. When Jesus said you are from beneath and I am from above to the Pharisees or Jewish religious leaders he was saying they were of earth and he (Jesus) was from above or from (the third) heaven. Jesus then went on with this contrast between the Jewish religious leaders and himself to say they were of this world system and that he was not of this world system. In this case Jesus was probably referring to especially the self sufficient or humanistic religious and moral aspects of this world system that characterized the Pharisees and contrasting it with himself and his God sufficient and dependant spirituality and values that were from heaven. Of course there are other aspects of the man sufficient and to some extent godless and satanically corrupted world system such as its economic, military, entertainment, social and political aspects but these were not what primarily characterized the Pharisees. Jesus then went on to say to the Jewish religious leaders the Pharisees that they would die in their sins unless they believed that he was the genuine Son of God, the Messiah of Israel and the Savior of the world etc. Jesus said this because these religious leaders as many of the Jews of their time were not looking to Jesus or any other candidate for Messiah to pay the substitutionary penalty for their sins after coming in human form from heaven and offering a God sufficient faith and spirituality.

# The Worlds Way

Instead the Pharisees were content to rely on a religion that was humanistic and man sufficient by good works or a perceived good nature that is part of the man sufficient world system and not salvation or redemption by blood of an innocent substitute and faith in him that in the case of Jesus is through a God sufficient sacrifice and object of faith. The scripture reference from Gospel of John 8 of the Lord Jesus Christ contrasting the Jewish religious leaders being part of the world system especially its religious aspect but Himself not of this world system but from above meaning from the Heavenly Father for his spirituality is as follows: And he (Jesus) said to them, You are from beneath; I am from above: you are of this world; I am not of this world. I said therefore to you, that you shall die in your sins: for if you believe not that I am he, you shall die in your sins. Gospel of John 8:23-24. In this chapter (verse 31) the Lord Jesus Christ predicts or prophesies that the time of his death on the cross was the judgment of this world. The Lord Jesus Christ could say that because His death on the cross was the payment for the sins of all the people of the world that was and is opposed to him and God. From Jesus' death on the cross we have the barrier of our sins which alienates us from the true and living God the heavenly Father and his fellowship at least potentially removed by the death of the sinless Son of God and God (the Son) come in the form of a perfect sinless man. Jesus could therefore pay the penalty under the law of death for sin as our substitute and still satisfy God with a just way to offer us salvation and eternal life. However we have to admit we are sinners and deserve the judgment of this world by ourselves and ask God in Jesus' name for his salvation through His Son Jesus Christ to obtain and realize this salvation, forgiveness and eternal life and freedom from judgment and condemnation.

Through Jesus' death the prince of this world the devil was also cast out from being the tyrant over the lives of believers in this world (earth) as we can live in victory and an overcoming life if we abide in Christ and walk in the Holy Spirit instead of living in the old and sinful nature that Satan can control. In this life believers in the Lord Jesus Christ, (true or born again Christians), have a choice to live in bondage to Satan or to live in spiritual freedom in the Lord Jesus Christ but this is definitely a struggle but God can give us strength for victory if we yield ourselves wholeheartedly to him. In the life to come for true Christians our old nature will be cast off and we will continuously effortlessly live in spiritual victory and freedom from the god of this world who will not have our old nature to get a foothold in our lives anymore. The successful death for our sins and rising from the dead of the Lord Jesus Christ assures us that He will ultimately and not too long from now come again to judge this world and take it over and reign here visibly and bind the devil and all the demons in hell for 1000 years and then forever. The scripture reference for the death for our sins of the Lord Jesus Christ as the means of the judgment of this world system and of the prince of this world the devil in the Gospel of John 12 is as follows: Jesus answered and said, This voice came not because of me, but for your sakes. Now is the judgment of this world: now shall the prince of this world be cast out. And I, if I be lifted up from the earth, will draw all men to me. Gospel of John 12:30-32. The Lord Jesus Christ says here in Gospel of John 15 that the true Christian shouldn't be surprised if the world system or people of this world system hate them because it hated him before it hated us. This world system or the people of this world system are those who are preoccupied with the things on earth and of time and sense and what they can get out of life for themselves.

## The Worlds Way

This is instead of people living for the things of eternity and heaven and God ward spirituality and what we can do first for God and the Lord Jesus Christ, then other people then ourselves. A main reason the world or people of the world hate Jesus and also the true Christian is because He and it should also be the case for believers live by higher more righteous and more selfless standards than the world. The Lord Jesus and we by our lives and to some extent by our words should try to get those of the world (people other than true or born again Christians) to stop living for themselves and admit their sins to God and invite the Lord Jesus Christ to be their personal Lord and Savior who died for their sins and rose again to give new life. The reason some even true Christians aren't too clearly hated by this world is that they seek to conform or be like this world and the things of this life and not live for God and Jesus and His word the Holy Bible and for heaven that the world isn't offended by them or their lives or words. However Christians shouldn't try to be needlessly offensive in our witness but some people will be offended even if we share the gospel or Christian message with much grace or love. Jesus goes on to say if we were of this world then the people of this world system would love us as being one of them. However Jesus says that true Christians are not of this world but that he has chosen us out of this world to separate us to Himself and God the Father as part of His Church which means a called out people from this world system. Because true Christians have been called out of this world system and no longer seek to live by its principles such as the religions, philosophies, entertainment, business, politics and science of this world then the world hates us. The scripture reference from Gospel of John 15 of the people of this world system hating the true Christian that doesn't live by the values of this world but warns those of the world to turn from its values to God through Jesus but that has been called out of this world to God and Jesus is as follows:

If the world hates you, ye know that it hated me before it hated you. If ye were of the world, the world would love his own: but because ye are not of the world, but I have chosen you out of the world, therefore the world hates you. Gospel of John 15:18-19. After the death of the Lord Jesus Christ, who was God come in the flesh, God had paid the penalty for the sins of all human beings that would justify us in God's sight if we stop trusting in ourselves for salvation and instead admit we are sinners in the sight of a holy but loving God and all we have to do is trust in God's perfect righteousness in the person of His Son Jesus Christ for salvation including his righteous death on the cross for our sins. This act of the Lord Jesus Christ also brings whoever trusts in Jesus as children of God and no longer under the power of Satan who is the god of this world system that includes all non-Christians and merely professing Christians who haven't trusted in the Lord Jesus Christ alone for salvation instead of still trusting themselves or their good works. After salvation through Jesus the only power Satan the god of this world can have over an individual is what we allow him to have by giving place to sin in our lives after the old or sinful nature. All this fact about the god of this world the devil being judged through Jesus' payment for our sins on the cross is one of the main things the Holy Spirit since he came to earth on Pentecost focuses on in his convicting work. The scripture reference of the convicting work of the Holy Spirit about the reality that the god of this world the devil is judged since the death of the Lord Jesus Christ on the cross for our sins is as follows: (Jesus said) Nevertheless I tell you the truth; It is expedient for you that I go away: for if I go not away, the Comforter (the Holy Spirit) will not come unto you; but if I depart, I will send him unto you.

## The Worlds Way

And when he is come, he will reprove the world of sin, and of righteousness, and of judgment: Of sin, because they believe not on me; Of righteousness, because I go to my Father, and ye see me no more; Of judgment, because the prince of this world is judged. Gospel of John 16:7-11. The Lord Jesus Christ said he gave his followers God's Word - the Bible including the New Testament and as a result the world system that is the political, business, military and entertainment and false scientific system have hated Christians because we are not of this world system as Jesus was not of this world system. Christians and Jesus are instead of God the Father and of God's heavenly and eternal kingdom through His Son Jesus Christ. God's Kingdom after Jesus' second coming will also rule visibly over this earth and then God will make a new heavens and new earth where his rule will totally be in force for His Son Jesus Christ and His people according to the Bible. The scripture reference from Gospel of John 17 of the Lord Jesus Christ saying that this world system or people of it would hate Christians because we hold to God's word instead of the teachings of men and that we are no longer of this world is as follows:

Jesus said I have given them thy word; and the world hath hated them, because they are not of the world, even as I am not of the world. Gospel of John 17:14 This passage is addressed to true Christians who have been quickened or made alive through faith in the Lord Jesus Christ and His death for our sins and resurrection from the dead to give us new life. This also resulted in us being freed from the bondage of the old nature that was dead (spiritually) or separated from God through trespasses and sins. The true Christian before we were saved also walked or lived in trespasses and sins which is after the course or ways and trends of the ungodly world system that is opposed or ignores God and His Son Jesus Christ and His Word - the Holy Bible and eternity, heaven and His spiritual things. This walking in trespasses and sins was also according to the prince of the power of the air or the devil or Satan which works against the unbeliever or even the old nature in the believer on earth in conjunction with the effects of the world system that both attract and cater to the fallen sinful nature of man. The prince of the power of the air (Satan) is the spirit that works in the children of disobedience or unbelievers. This scripture says we as Christians were unbelievers before we were saved through the Lord Jesus Christ and when we were still unbelievers we had our conversation or manner or practices in life in the lusts or desires of the flesh (fallen and godless human nature). We were then fulfilling the desires of the flesh and the mind that were opposed to or put in a higher place than desiring God or His Son Jesus Christ or His Word - the Holy Bible or His Holy Spirit. Our indulging in the temptations of the world system and of the devil fed these desires of the flesh. For this reason before we trusted in the Lord Jesus Christ we were then children of or under (God's) wrath even as others (who have still not trusted in the Lord Jesus Christ for salvation). The scripture reference from Ephesians 2 of the world system and its attractions and its relation to the devil and the fallen fleshly nature of man in causing people to sin before or without trusting in the Lord Jesus Christ for salvation and getting His new godly nature is as follows: And you hath he quickened, who were dead in trespasses and sins; Wherein in time past ye walked according to the course of this world, according to the prince of the power of the air, the spirit that now works in the children of disobedience: Among who also we all had our conversation in times past in the lusts of our flesh, fulfilling the desires of the flesh and of the mind; and were by nature the children of wrath, even as others. Ephesians 2:1-3.

# The Worlds Way

In Revelation 11 one of God's holy angels made an exclamation at the last of the trumpet judgments which will probably be near the end of the first half of the 7 year tribulation. Even though this statement by the angel is only near the end of the first half of the tribulation, he in his statement is clearly looking to the end of the tribulation when the Lord Jesus Christ will come from heaven with his holy angels and saints of previous ages including all church age saints or born again Christians to set up his kingdom over all the earth and remove the devil who has led the kingdom of this world system since the fall of man in the Garden of Eden. The antichrist and the false prophet who will lead the last form of the kingdoms of the world of a global government and global economy and religion etc. will also be removed by the Lord Jesus Christ at his second coming at the end of the tribulation. At that time the times of the Gentiles in which Israel is under control of non-Jewish national powers as well as the time from the fall of man in which mankind was ruled by mostly ungodly men and some women usually in the form of nations or tribes will end. This times of the Gentiles will then be replaced by God directly ruling through His Son and Anointed One Jesus of Nazareth over all the people and nations of the world for 1000 years on this earth and then for eternity on the new earth and heavens and New Jerusalem. It is somewhat unpopular to unsaved people who have their heart in this world system that is directed by the things of time and sense and self-centeredness. However God's people in this age true Christians who have a new nature in Christ Jesus through faith in Jesus' death for our sins and resurrection from the dead to give us new life should live instead for God's Millennial then eternal Kingdom that is focused on heaven, eternity and spiritual things and seeking foremost what pleases God then after this to please our neighbor as ourselves.

*Save The Family*

The scripture reference in Revelation 11 of the angelic announcement of the Lord Jesus Christ to end the kingdoms of the world dominated by Satan and other demons and replace it with God's Kingdom through Jesus Christ starting at the end of the tribulation at Jesus' second coming in Revelation 11 is as follows: And the seventh angel sounded and there were great voices in heaven, saying, The kingdoms of this world are become the kingdoms of our Lord, and of his Christ; and he shall reign forever and ever. Revelation 11:15.

# CHAPTER VIII

## The

## Rainbow Covenant

Ours is not an age that desires to make long-term commitments. The covenant of marriage is often avoided, and vows that are made lack the permanence and commitment of former days. Guarantees are given for a very short period. Contracts are often vaguely worded or are undermined by loopholes and fine print. Strangely, Christians seem to think that clear, contractual agreements are somehow unspiritual, especially between two believers. 'A man should be as good as his word,' we are told. And so he should. It is interesting to observe that the infinite, all-powerful, changeless God of the universe has chosen to deal with men in the form of covenants. The Noahic Covenant of Genesis chapter 9 is the first biblical covenant of the Bible. While the word 'covenant' appears in Genesis 6:18, it refers to the Noahic Covenant of chapter 9. This Noahic Covenant is important to us for a number of reasons. The Noahic Covenant, in addition to the fact that it is still in force today, also provides us with a pattern for all of the other biblical covenants. As we come to understand this covenant, we will more fully appreciate the significance of all of the covenants, and especially the New Covenant instituted by our Lord Jesus Christ. Technically, Genesis 8:20-22 is not a promise which God gave to Noah. Rather it is a purpose confirmed in the heart of God. And the Lord smelled the soothing aroma; and the Lord said to Himself, 'I will never again curse the ground on account of man, for the intent of man's heart is evil from his youth; and I will never again destroy every living things as I have done' (Genesis 8:21).

These are not words spoken to Noah, they are purposes reaffirmed in the mind of God. Covenant theologians place much emphasis on two or three theological covenants: the covenant of works, the covenant of grace, and the covenant of redemption. All of these covenants, while they may well be 'biblical' in essence, are implicit, rather than explicit. Covenant theologians usually tend to emphasize these implied theological covenants at the expense of the clearly biblical covenants, such as the Noahic Covenant. On the other hand, dispensational theologians often stress the biblical covenants and disparage the theological covenants. In Genesis chapters 8 and 9 both elements are to be found. The eternal purpose of God to save men was made long before the days of Noah (cf. Ephesians 1:4; 3:11; II Thessalonians 2:13; II Timothy 1:9, etc.). What we find in Genesis 8:20-22 is not the creation of God's purpose to save men, but the confirmation of that purpose in history. Just as God reaffirmed His purpose here, such recommitment is often good for men as well (cf. Philippians 3:8-16). The covenant of God with Himself was occasioned by the sacrifices offered up by Noah (Genesis 8:20). God's resolve was to never again destroy the earth by a flood (cf. 9:11). I understand the words, "... I will never again curse the ground on account of many..." (verse 21), to be parallel with the following expression, "... and I will never again destroy every living thing as I have done" (verse 21). The reason for God's resolve is based upon the nature of man: "For the intent of man's heart is evil from his youth" (Genesis 8:21). Righteous Noah (6:9) will soon be found naked in a drunken stupor (9:21). No matter how many times the earth's slate is wiped clean by a flood, the problem will remain if but one man exists. The problem is within man—it is his sinful nature.

## The Rainbow Covenant

His predisposition toward sin is not learned, it is innate—he is "evil from his youth." As a result, a full restoration must begin with a new man. This is what God historically purposed to accomplish. This purpose is partially expressed in verse 22: "While the earth remains, seedtime and harvest, and cold and heat, and summer and winter, and day and night shall not cease." Here (Genesis 9:1) and there (Genesis 1:28) God blessed His creatures and told them to be fruitful and multiply. Here (Genesis 9:3) and there (Genesis 1:29-30) God prescribed the food man could eat. There are differences, however, which indicate that the new beginning is to be different from the old. God pronounced the original creation 'good' (cf. 1:21, 31). The world of Noah's day received no such commendation, for the men who possessed it were sinful (8:21). Adam was charged to subdue the earth and to rule over the animal kingdom (1:28). Noah was given no such command. Instead, God placed in the animals a fear of man by which man could achieve a measure of control over them. (The reason my dog obeys me—when he does—is because he fears me.) While Adam and his contemporaries seem to have been vegetarians (Genesis 1:29-30; cf. 9:3), Noah and his descendants could eat flesh (9:3-4). There was, however, one stipulation. They could not eat the blood of the animal, for the life of the animal was in its blood. This was to teach man not only that God values life, but that He owns it. God allows man to take the life of animals in order to survive, but they must not eat the blood. One may puzzle that flesh could be eaten after the flood, but not before (or so it seems). It may be that conditions on the earth so changed that protein was now necessary for life. More likely, man must be brought to the realization that, because of his sin, he could only live by the death of another.

Man lives by the death of animals. Most important of all, man is taught to reverence life. Men before the fall were obviously men of violence (cf. Genesis 6:11) who, like Cain (Genesis 4:8), and Lamech (Genesis 4:23-24), had no regard for human life. This is more emphatically stated in verses 5 and 6 of chapter 9: And surely I will require your lifeblood; from every beast I will require it. And from every man, from every man's brother I will require the life of man. Whoever sheds man's blood, by man his blood shall be shed, for in the image of God He made man. The life of man was precious and belonged to God. It was God's to give and His alone to take. Animals which shed man's blood must be put to death (verse 5, cf. Exodus 21:28,29). Men who willfully take the life of another must be put to death 'by man' (verse 6; cf. Numbers 35:33).[98] In addition to murder, suicide is prohibited by God's command in these verses. Life belongs to God—not only the life of animals and of others, but our own as well. We must realize that suicide is taking our life into our own hands when God says it belongs to Him. In the words of Job, "The Lord gave, and the Lord has taken away" (Job 1:21). This passage seems to shed light on the controversial subject of abortion also. Man is not to shed the blood of man. The life of man is in the blood (Genesis 9:4; Leviticus 17:11). Aside from many other considerations, must we not conclude that at the time a fetus has blood, it has life? Must we not also acknowledge that to shed this blood, to destroy this fetus, is to violate God's command and to be subject to the death penalty? Man is created in the image of God (Genesis 1:27; 9:6). In view of this fact, murder is much more than an act of hostility against man—it is an affront to God. To attack man is to attack God in whose image he was created. We have said that murder is sin because life belongs to God. We have also shown that murder must be severely dealt with because the victim is a person created in the divine image.

## The Rainbow Covenant

One further reason for capital punishment remains in this passage: man must shed the blood of the murderer because he is also a part of the divine image. "Whoever sheds man's blood, by man his blood shall be shed, for in the image of God He made man" (verse 6). God did not take the life of Cain when he killed his brother, Abel. I believe God allowed Cain to live so that we could see the consequences of allowing the murderer to go free. Lamech could kill a young lad for what may have been a mere insult and boast of it (Genesis 4:23-24). The men who died in the flood were men of violence (6:11). God did punish sin, but He delayed the execution until the days of the flood so that we could learn the high price of allowing the murderer to go free. Now that all mankind had perished because of his sin, God could require society to take the life of the murderer. In this act of capital punishment, man would act on behalf of God—he would reflect the moral image of God, namely, His indignation and sentence upon the murderer. Man (and by this I understand Moses to be referring to society and its governmental agency) is required to execute the murderer to reflect the moral purity of His Creator. Government acts in God's behalf in punishing the evildoer and rewarding those who do good:

Let every person be in subjection to the governing authorities. For there is no authority except from God, and those which exist are established by God. Therefore he who resists authority has opposed the ordinance of God; and they who have opposed will receive condemnation upon themselves. For rulers is not a cause of fear for good behaviors but for evil. Do you want to have no fear of authority? Do what is good, and you will have praise from the same; for it is a minister of God to you for good. But if you do what is evil, be afraid; for it does not bear the sword for nothing; for it is a minister of Gods an avenger who brings wrath upon the one who practices evil (Romans 13:1-4).

The 'sword' which Paul mentions in verse 4 is the sword used by the executioner to carry out capital punishment. Our Lord Himself gave testimony to the fact that government had been given the task of executing law-breakers: Pilate therefore said to Him 'You do not speak to me? Do You not know that I have authority to release You, and I have authority to crucify You?' Jesus answered, 'You would have no authority over Me, unless it had been given you from above; for this reason, he who delivered Me up to you has the greater sin' (John 19:10-11). The command concerning capital punishment is, I believe, the cornerstone of any society of sinful men. The animal kingdom is to be controlled, to a great extent, by means of their fear of man (9:2). Man's sinful tendencies, also, are kept in check by his fear of the consequences. Any society which loses its reverence for life cannot endure long. For this reason, God instituted capital punishment as a gracious restraint upon man's sinful tendency toward violence. Because of this, mankind can live in relative peace and security until God's Messiah has dealt the death blow to sin. And so a new age has dawned. Not an age of naive optimism, but one to be lived by clear commands. And, as we shall see in the following verses, one that has a hope for the future. God's covenant with Noah and his descendants displays many of the characteristics of subsequent covenants which God had made with man. For this reason, we shall highlight some of the covenant's more obvious features. The sovereignty of God is clearly seen in this covenant. While some ancient covenants were the result of negotiation, this one was not. God initiated the covenant as an outward expression of His purpose revealed in Genesis 3:20-22. God dictated the terms of the covenant to Noah, and there was no discussion. A friend of mine owned a car that was 'on its last leg.' With my encouragement, he went to a car lot to find something more dependable.

## The Rainbow Covenant

He found a car which showed promise but decided to give the matter more deliberation. When he got into his old car to leave, it wouldn't start. As you can imagine, my friend was in no position to bargain. He took the other car without any negotiation concerning the price. That was precisely the situation of Noah. And I might add, would we dare to question God's terms today? I think not! The Noahic Covenant was made with Noah and all successive generations: "And God said, 'This is the sign of the covenant which I am making between Me and you and every living creation that is with you, for all successive generations;'" ( Genesis 9:12). This covenant will remain in force until the time when our Lord returns to the earth to cleanse it by fire (II Peter 3:10). This is a universal covenant. While some covenants involve a small number, this particular covenant includes "all flesh." That is, all living creatures, including man and animals: Now behold, I Myself do establish My covenant with you, and with your descendants after you; and with every living creature that is with you, the birds, the cattle, and every beast of the earth with you; of all that comes out of the ark, even every beast of the earth (Genesis 9:9,10). The Noahic Covenant is an unconditional covenant. Some covenants were contingent upon both parties carrying out certain stipulations. Such was the case of the Mosaic covenant. If Israel kept the law of God, they would experience the blessings and prosperity of God. If not, they would be expelled from the land (Deuteronomy 28). The blessings of the Noahic covenant were not conditional. God would give regularity of seasons and would not destroy the earth by a flood simply because He said so. While certain commands were given to mankind in verses 1-7, these are not viewed as conditions to the covenant. They are technically not included as a part of the covenant.

This covenant was God's promise never again to destroy the earth by a flood: "and I will remember My covenant, which is between Me and you and every living creature of all flesh; and never again shall the water become a flood to destroy all flesh" (Genesis 9:15). God will destroy the earth by fire (II Peter 3:10), but only after salvation has been purchased by the Messiah and the elect are removed, even as Noah was protected from the wrath of God.

**The sign of the Noahic Covenant is the rainbow:** I set My bow in the cloud, and it shall be for a sign of a covenant between Me and the earth. And it shall come about, when I bring a cloud over the earth, that the bow shalt be seen in the cloud and I will remember My covenant, which is between Me and you and every living creature of all flesh; and never again shall the water become a flood to destroy all flesh (Genesis 9:13-15). Every covenant has its accompanying sign. The sign of the Abrahamic Covenant is circumcision (Genesis 17:15-27); that of the Mosaic Covenant is the observance of the Sabbath day (Exodus 20:8-11; 31:12-17). The "sign" of the rainbow is appropriate. It consists of the reflection of the rays of the sun in the particles of moisture in the clouds. The water which destroyed the earth causes the rainbow. Also, the rainbow appears at the end of a storm. So this sign assures man that the storm of God's wrath (in a flood) is over. Most interesting is the fact that the rainbow is not designed so much for man's benefit (in this text, at least) but for God's. God said that the rainbow would cause Him to remember His covenant with man. What a comfort to know that God's faithfulness is our guarantee.

## The Rainbow Covenant

**Conclusions and Application**

For the Israelites who first received this revelation from God, the Noahic Covenant gave reasons for a number of the rules laid down in the Mosiac Law. The laws pertaining to capital punishment, for example, found their origin and explanation in Genesis chapter 9. The meticulous matters concerning blood take on added meaning in the light of this chapter. The prophets of old referred to the Noahic Covenant as well. Isaiah reminded the nation, Israel, of God's faithfulness in keeping the Noahic Covenant: "'For this is like the days of Noah to Me; when I swore that the waters of Noah should not flood the earth again, so I have sworn that I will not be angry with you, nor will I rebuke you. For the mountains may be removed and the hills may shake, but My loving kindness will not be removed from you, and My covenant of peace will not be shaken,' says the Lord who has compassion on you" (Isaiah 54:9-10). At the time of Isaiah's writing there seemed to be little grounds for hope as a nation. Isaiah reminded the nation that their hope was as sure as the Word of God. God's promise of coming redemption should be viewed in the light of His faithfulness in keeping His covenant with Noah and his descendants. The language of Genesis chapter nine was employed by Hosea to assure God's people of their restoration:"In that day I will also make a covenant for them with the beasts of the field, the birds of the sky, and the creeping things of the ground. And I will abolish the bow, the sword, and war from the land, and will make them lie down in safety" (Hosea 2:18). Jeremiah also spoke of God's future blessings by reminding men of God's faithfulness in keeping the Noahic Covenant:

"Thus says the Lord, Who gives the sun for light by day, and the fixed order of the moon and the stars for light by night, Who stirs up the sea so that its waves roar; the Lord of hosts is His name:

'If this fixed order departs from before Me,' declares the Lord, 'then the offspring of Israel also shall cease from being a nation before Me forever.' Thus says the Lord, 'If the heavens above can be measured, and the foundations of the earth searched out below, then I will also cast off all the offspring of Israel for all that they have done,' declares the Lord" (Jeremiah 31:35-37; cf. also 33:20-26; Psalm 89:30-37). The Israelites could look forward to the salvation which God would bring to pass. We can look backward to that which God has accomplished by His Messiah, the Lord Jesus Christ. While Israel awaits the complete fulfillment of God's covenant in the Millennium, they may do so with confidence in the God Who keeps His commitments. We, too, as Christians can be fully assured of God's faithfulness. The Noahic Covenant in many ways foreshadowed the New Covenant. Consequently, the New Covenant fulfilled much that the Noahic Covenant anticipated. The shedding of blood took on new meaning in the Noahic Covenant. The shedding of Christ's blood at Calvary suddenly brought the ninth chapter of Genesis into full focus. Since all of the biblical covenants culminate in the New Covenant which greatly overshadows them, let us take a few moments to compare the features of the New Covenant with the Noahic Covenant. The New Covenant is promised in Jeremiah 31:30-34: But everyone will die for his own iniquity; each man who eats the sour grapes, his teeth will be set on edge.

## The Rainbow Covenant

'Behold, days are coming,' declares the Lord, 'when I will make a new covenant with the house of Israel and with the house of Judah, not like the covenant which I made with their fathers in the day I took them by the hand to bring them out of the land of Egypt, My covenant which they broke, although I was a husband to them,' declares the Lord. 'But this is the covenant which I will make with the house of Israel after those days,' declares the Lord, 'I will put My law within them, and on their heart I will write it; and I will be their God, and they shall be My people. And they shall not teach again, each man his neighbor and each man his brother saying, 'Know the Lord,' for they shall all know Me, from the least of them to the greatest of them,' declares the Lord, 'for I will forgive their iniquity, and their sin I will remember no more' (Jeremiah 31:30-34). Our Lord instituted this covenant by His death on the cross of Calvary. The sign of the covenant is the Lord's table: And while they were eating, Jesus took some bread, and after a blessing, He broke it and gave it to the disciples, and said, 'Take, eat; this is My body.' And He took a cup and gave thanks, and gave it to them, saying, 'Drink from it, all of you; for this is My blood of the covenant, which is to be shed on behalf of many for forgiveness of sins. But I say to you, I will not drink of this fruit of the vine from now on until that day when I drink it new with you in My Father's kingdom' (Matthew 26:26-29). The writer to the Hebrews stressed that the New Covenant superseded the Old (Mosaic) Covenant and is vastly superior to it. The New Covenant, like the Noahic, was initiated by God, and it was accomplished by Him. While all flesh have benefited from the common grace of God promised in the Noahic Covenant, only those who are 'in Christ' benefit from the blessings of the New Covenant. It is the New Covenant 'in His blood,' that is experienced by those who have trusted in the shed blood of Christ, the Lamb of God, for the forgiveness of sins and the gift of eternal life.

Our Lord said to his followers: Jesus therefore said to them, 'Truly, truly, I say to you, unless you eat the flesh of the Son of Man and drink His blood, you have no life in yourselves. He who eats My flesh and drinks My blood has eternal life; and I will raise him up on the last day. For My flesh is true food, and My blood is true drink' (John 6:53-55). By this He meant that one must not only acknowledge Christ's deity and the death that He died for sinners, but must also make this a vital part of his life by trusting only in Christ for salvation. The only condition for entering into the blessings of the New Covenant is the expression of personal faith in Christ by receiving Him: But as many as received Him, to them He gave the right to become children of God, even to those who believe in His name (John 1:12). And the witness is this, which God has given us eternal life, and this life is in His Son. He who has the Son has the life; he who does not have the Son of God does not have the life (I John 5:11-12). Like the Noahic Covenant, those who are under the New Covenant have no need to fear the future outbreak of divine wrath. While the Noahic Covenant guaranteed all flesh that God would never again destroy all life by a flood, the New Covenant assures man that he will not face the outpouring of divine wrath through other means, such as fire (II Peter 3:10). And the witness is this, which God has given us eternal life, and this life is in His Son. He who has the Son has the life; he who does not have the Son of God does not have the life (I John 5:11-12). Like the Noahic Covenant, those who are under the New Covenant have no need to fear the future outbreak of divine wrath. While the Noahic Covenant guaranteed all flesh that God would never again destroy all life by a flood, the New Covenant assures man that he will not face the outpouring of divine wrath through other means, such as fire (II Peter 3:10 ... and to Jesus, the mediator of a new covenant, and to the sprinkled blood, which speaks better than the blood of Abel (Hebrews 12:24).

## The Rainbow Covenant

The covenant made between God and the patriarch Noah immediately after the flood was one of a series of covenants entered into by the creator with his creatures. This is important since, although restricted in a sense, it is the basis upon which the three great covenants of the Bible—the Abrahamic, the Law, and the New have their standing. Without the carrying into effect of the provisions of the covenant with Noah, the other three could not be fulfilled. The background of the flood is one of the amazing stories of the Bible. It tells us about the angels who attempted to father a race of men with human women. The apostles Peter and Jude refer to it. In 2 Peter 2:4 they are called the "angels that sinned" and in Jude 6 the angels which kept not their first estate. The account in Genesis 6:1-4 describes a time when mankind began noticeably to increase in the earth; some of the sons of God, the angels, assumed human form and took wives of "the daughters of men. They abandoned their spiritual state to concentrate on the possibilities offered on earth. Possibly they were influenced by Satan in a plot to defeat the death sentence and so outwit God by introducing, non-Adamic life into the human race. Their offspring was a race whose conduct instituted a reign of terror in the earth. This led the Almighty eventually to destroy the entire community in the great flood and start again. Genesis 6:3 appears to suggest that the Lord placed a limitation on the situation. God had given his angels the opportunity to rule over the antediluvian world and he would not permit them to continue longer. A span of one hundred twenty years was decreed before the catastrophe would occur. It gave an opportunity for repentance and undoubtedly it was during this time that Noah was, as asserted by Peter, a preacher of righteousness (2 Peter 2:5).

The word rendered "giants" in Genesis 6:4 is *nephilim*. Genesis 6:4 apparently says the nephilim were already in the earth before the progeny of the fallen angels were born. Thus, the word "nephilim" should probably be reserved for the giants among the male descendants of Adam. Another view is the word "nephilim" refers to the angels themselves rather than the progeny. It is a contraction of the Hebrew words *naphal* and *elohim* or "fallen gods."} This was apparently the name given to the offspring resulting from these unnatural unions. The word "giants" used for *nephilim* in the *King James* Bible is derived from the Greek Septuagint which adopted the Greek *gigantos* in that translation leading to the English words "gigantic" and "giant." Next we are told, "After that, when the sons of God came in unto the daughters of men, and they bare children to them: the same were the mighty men that were of old, the men of renown. Some believe that the object of the angels was to impart to mankind the eternal life which Adam had lost. The birth of the *nephilim* continued during this period of time while the condition of things persisted. But something went terribly wrong with the fallen angels' plan. Instead of bringing happiness, we are told the *nephilim* became tyrants bringing death and violence and oppressing mankind. The Apocryphal Books of Jubilees and Enoch describe in some detail the terrible tyranny which mankind suffered at the hands of the *nephilim*. The fifth chapter of Jubilees is almost word-for-word identical with the Genesis 6 account but it adds the deeds of the *nephilim*. The language in Genesis 6:4 is restrained only stating that they were mighty men of renown. Most likely it was an evil renown for they were known for their wickedness and ferocity.

## The Rainbow Covenant

The Scriptures indicate that angels do not have all knowledge and do have limitations. 1 Peter 1:12 and Mark 13:32 tell us that some aspects of God's plan are hidden from them. It appears that in their scheming and planning, the fallen angels overlooked one vital factor: human intelligence is distinct from the instinct which governs the lower creatures. Man is empowered with faculties possessed by no other earthly creature: an appreciation of God, reverence, loyalty, love, the instinct for worship, and powers of reasoning on the past and future. These are a gift of God, bestowed only by him and are attributes implanted by God at the time of man's creation. When God created man, he gave man an unseen bond of power, which made Adam both a man and a son of God. The angel's offspring lacked that quality that God gave to Adam. The angel's offspring introduced an element of disorder into the divine creation. These offspring, who perished in the flood, were an illicit race since they were not pure descendants of Adam and, therefore, can have no resurrection. The Scriptures clearly teach that only those who die in Adam are made alive in Christ. In the future Adams progeny will awake to an opportunity of returning to and becoming reconciled with God the hearts of the angels offspring were set on wickedness and every form of evil. When God looked down, he saw only that "the wickedness of man was great in the earth, and that every imagination of the thoughts of his heart was only evil continually (Genesis 6:5,). So the LORD said, I will blot out man whom I have created from the face of the ground, man and beast and creeping things and birds of the air, for I am sorry that I have made them" (Genesis 6:7,). The great deluge which was prophesied and preached by Noah for a hundred and twenty years then took place.

As a result, the earth's surface became desolated by this convulsion of nature. No human life survived, except those who drifted in the ark at the mercy of the waters. Noah, seeing the desolation before him, possibly thought that God would have to periodically blot out all earth's achievements and make a fresh start to preserve righteousness and truth. What would become of the promise made to mother Eve much earlier, and cherished through the centuries by the family of Noah, that the seed of the woman would bruise the serpents head? Noah might have wondered what guarantee there would be that this destruction would not be repeated. To answer such questions, and to commence a definition of Gods gracious purposes and the principles of his plan, God made an unconditional covenant with Noah. In Genesis 8:20 we are told that Noah, after his safe deliverance from the destruction that had engulfed the world, built an altar and offered burnt offerings upon it of every clean beast and every clean bird. Noah had been told, "Of every clean beast thou shall take to you seven and seven, the male and his female; and of the beasts that are not clean two, the male and his female: of the birds also of the heavens, seven and seven, male and female, to keep seed alive upon the face of all the earth" (Genesis 7:2,3, *ASV*) That is why a clean animal and a clean bird could be sacrificed and still not jeopardize the reproduction of that species after the flood. When God smelled the sweet savor of Noah's sacrifice, he declared and ratified his covenant with Noah. It was an important occasion, for a new world was about to be born. The evil of the past world was blotted out from Gods sight and mankind was clean in a cleansed world and able to make a fresh start with divine favor: "Jehovah smelled the sweet savor; and Jehovah said in his heart, I will not again curse the ground any more for man's sake, [and] neither will I again smite any more everything living, as I have done" (Genesis 8:21,).

# The Rainbow Covenant

It was a special occasion for a new world, one that was to witness all the strange events associated with the divine plan of salvation. The whole future of that world rested upon Noah and his three sons gathered around the altar. The covenant with Noah was established to record the divine pledge that never again would the earth be destroyed. Mankind and animals could go about their respective commissions to multiply and fill the earth without fear of another universal catastrophe. The terms of the pledge are given in Genesis 8:21,22 and 9:11-16. This covenant was not only made with Noah, his three sons, Shem, Ham, Japheth, and their children, but also with the lower creation. The great creator pledged faith with the birds of the air, the cattle of the pasture land, and even the wild beasts of the jungle. We come across divine care for the animal world in Jonah 4:11: "And should not I spare Nineveh, that great city, wherein are more than six score thousand persons and also much cattle? Our Lord confirmed Gods care for animals with his words in Luke 12:6: Are not five sparrows sold for two farthings, and not one of them is forgotten before God? "The terms of the covenant were given by the Almighty and the little group accepted their commission. In the divine plan they were to be the progenitors of the original Adamic race from whom would be taken many years later the future ministers of reconciliation between God and mankind. But that could not take place until later; after the greater Abrahamic Covenant had been made The covenant with Noah is like the Abrahamic Covenant which followed 427 years later. It is an unconditional covenant because God committed to it without a if condition, as was the case with the Law Covenant at Mt. Sinai. The covenant was made with Noah as the chief contracting party, but not because of anything he undertook to do in the future. It was because of the faith and loyalty Noah had manifested in the past, as was the case with Abraham.

The Abrahamic Covenant is Gods formal guarantee to bring into being a "seed, " and through that seed to bless all the families of the earth. The covenant with Noah is Gods formal guarantee to preserve the earth and all its processes from any further destruction, so that it may remain forever a suitable and fitting environment for the operations of that "seed" and a home for the blessed families of the earth. The fulfillment of the Abrahamic Covenant requires a perpetually fertile earth for those blessed under this covenant. The covenant with Noah guarantees such an everlasting earth. The Scriptural basis for this is in the ninth chapter of Genesis which details the covenant of Noah. Also in Ecclesiastes 1:4 we are assured that "the earth abides forever" and that it will not be destroyed again by a flood. The covenant with Noah defines for us the physical principles upon which the "present evil world will pass away and be replaced by "the world to come, wherein dwells righteousness" (Galatians 1:4; Hebrews 2:5; 2 Peter 3:13). Today, in a world where men's hearts are "failing them" for fear that human life will become extinct by atomic warfare and that complete desolation will come, it is comforting to remember Gods covenant with Noah. Here we find divine assurance that such a dreadful climax to human history from another flood will never be reached. In his own due time, and by the exercise of his supreme power, God will intervene and restrain the forces of evil before they can destroy mankind. Our Lord Jesus makes mention of this when he said that if the great time of trouble continued, "there should no flesh be saved: but for the elects sake those days shall be shortened" (Matthew 24:22). It appears from the narrative that the sight of the rainbow in the clouds after the flood was a new phenomenon. It was a sign from God that he would never again desolate the world by a flood.

## The Rainbow Covenant

The rainbow would have had no meaning if Noah had seen it before. Possibly there was no rain as we know it before the flood and therefore no rainbow in the sky. If light from the sun was diffused by a kind of water canopy surrounding earth, no rainbow could be seen even around a waterfall. The rainbow seen in the clouds must have made a tremendous impression on the minds of Noah and his family. Eventually, as mankind spread over the face of the earth, they took with them the idea that a rainbow was a sign of assurance, of security and a token of Gods faithfulness (Isaiah 54:9,10). It gives us a connection between the covenant made with Noah and the much later fulfillment of divine promises in the protection and salvation of his people. The rainbow is a witness of this covenant. Genesis 9:12 states that it is a covenant for perpetual generations and in verse 16 observing the rainbow will cause God to remember the everlasting covenant." There could not be a more beautiful or fitting token that there shall never again be a flood that sweeps away all flesh and destroys all the land. The bow rose from the rain of the very waters that destroyed the earth, but were now used to seal Gods original intent in having created the earth. By saving Noah and the cargo of animals, God was making a statement before all the myriads of angels who were watching. We are told that we are a spectacle unto the angels (1 Corinthians 4:9). A rainbow is caused by the rays of the sun reflecting from falling raindrops at a particular angle to the eye of the spectator. A beautiful arch of reflected and refracted light is formed for every eye. Since there is no longer a veil of water around the earth, such a flood will never be repeated. Interestingly, while the rainbow spans a continuous spectrum of colors, humans typically see in the rainbow seven distinct colors. These may also have spiritual significance. The seven colors are red, orange, yellow, green, blue, indigo, and violet.

Seven represents perfection, so the rainbow might picture Gods perfect plan. When all the colors of the rainbow are combined together, they give us white sunlight. White is the symbol of purity and the righteousness of Christ, just as black, the opposite of white, pictures sin. The seven colors with possible spiritual significance contained in the rainbow are in the order of the letters ROY G BIV:

**Red** is the color of blood and represents the shed blood of Jesus given for many for the remission of sins to meet the demands of perfect justice. It is the color that stands for the ransom paid. We are told that without the shedding of blood there is no remission of sins.

**Orange** is a combination of yellow, symbolic of Gods divine nature, together with red, symbolic of Christ's sacrifice. The resulting color of orange is symbolic of Gods perfect plan and purpose for mankind. Orange could show us Gods favor to mankind.

**Yellow** is the color of gold. It reminds us of the things pertaining to the divine and its nature.

**Green** is a combination of blue and yellow. It is the yellow of Gods power and the blue of Jesus' faithfulness that will give everlasting life to all people of the earth. Therefore, green could stand for longevity, eternity, or earthly prosperity.

**Blue** could represent faithfulness. It reminds us of Gods faithfulness. As the blue color of the heavens does not change, so also with God: "I am the LORD, I change not" (Malachi 3:6).

**Indigo**, the color between blue and violet, is rather a blue with a reddish cast to it. This could represent our Lord Jesus Christ as a propitiation for our sins; Jesus' blood (red) through faith (blue) (1 John 2:1,2; Romans 3:25). Both indigo and violet also represent royalty.

## The Rainbow Covenant

**Violet**, the color in the rainbow with the shortest wavelength, is considered a shade of purple, according to English usage, because it lies between the colors blue and red on the color wheel. True purple is not found in the rainbow because it is a combination of two non-adjacent colors of the rainbow: blue symbolizing Gods faithfulness and red representing the ransom. Purple is the color of kings and symbolic of royalty. Violet, also lying between blue and red, could also represent royalty. The rainbow is the divine promise that never again shall there be such a calamity as a flood to destroy all flesh. The covenant with Noah provided the necessary guarantee that this earth, with all its wealth of minerals, vegetable, and animal life will continue its course into the ages of glory and infinite future. All who give themselves to God, whether in this age under the Abrahamic Covenant, or in the next age under the New Covenant, can do so in full assurance, that having been reconciled to God, they will go on into eternity resting in the faithfulness of God and of his eternal purpose. He who has redeemed the world shall be its lord and king. The dominion shall not be given to other people nor left to others. When the Messiah shall have conquered and put down all insubordination and everything contrary to the divine will, then the kingdom shall be delivered to God, that he may be all in all (1 Corinthians 15:28). See….the rainbow color represents a covering of death and destruction that GOD promise would happen based on future sins of man. This destruction being fire brim destruction, meaning the world would be destroyed by fire and no longer by water. When you in the Homosexual community take on these colors as your symbol of life to represent togetherness...peace, love and safety, you need to understand that you put yourselves under a symbol of death & destruction that GOD declared that would be upon the earth in its last days.

## Save The Family

Just look at what is happening in your communities today. In the first study to look at the consequences of anti-gay prejudice for mortality, researchers found that lesbian, gay, and bisexual (LGBT) individuals who lived in communities with high levels of anti-gay prejudice have a shorter life expectancy of 12 years on average compared with their peers in the least prejudiced communities."Our findings indicate that sexual minorities living in communities with higher levels of prejudice die sooner than sexual minorities living in low-prejudice communities, and that these effects are independent of established risk factors for mortality, including household income, education, gender, ethnicity, and age, as well as the average income and education level of residents in the communities where the respondents lived". "In fact, the results for prejudice were comparable to life expectancy differences that have been observed between individuals with and without a high school education." In order to examine the relationship between prejudice and mortality, the researchers constructed a measure capturing the average level of anti-gay prejudice in the communities where LGBT individuals lived, beginning in 1988, using data on prejudicial attitudes from the General Social Survey, one of The primary sources of social indicator data in the social sciences. This information on sexual orientation and community-level prejudice was then linked longitudinally to mortality data via the National Death Index, through 2008. Thus, the authors were able to examine whether mortality risk differed for LGBT individuals who lived in communities that were characterized by high versus low levels of prejudice. By the end of the study, 92% of LGBT respondents living in low-prejudice communities were still alive; in contrast, only 78% of the LGBT respondents living in high-prejudice communities were still alive.

The authors also found that suicide, homicide/violence, and cardiovascular diseases were all substantially elevated among sexual minorities in high-prejudice communities. LGBT respondents living in high-prejudice communities died of suicide on average at age 37.5, compared to age 55.7 for those living in low-prejudice communities, a striking 18-year difference. Homicide and violence-related deaths are one of the most direct links between hostile community attitudes and death, and results indicated that homicide rates were over three times more likely to occur in high-prejudice communities than in low-prejudice communities. Of the deaths in high-prejudice communities, 25% were due to cardiovascular disease, compared to 18.6% of deaths in the low-prejudice communities. "Psychosocial stressors are strongly linked to cardiovascular risk, and this kind of stress may represent an indirect pathway through which prejudice contributes to mortality. Discrimination, prejudice, and social marginalization create several unique demands on stigmatized individuals that are stress-inducing," said Dr. Hatzenbuehler. Currently there are slightly more than 30,000 suicides annually 83 suicides per day or 1 suicide every 17 minutes, with 11 of every 100,000 Americans killing themselves. Suicide is the eleventh leading cause of death. Males complete suicide at a rate four times that of females. However, females attempt suicide three times more often than males. Groups at particular risk include people with depression, schizophrenia, drug and/or chemical dependency, and panic disorder. Feelings of hopelessness are found to be more predictive of suicide risk than a diagnosis of depression. Socially isolated individuals are generally found to be at a higher risk for suicide. The vast majority of individuals who are suicidal often display clues and warning signs.

*Save The Family*

This is not the world being destroyed by fire as to the Rainbow Covenant of GOD, but this suicide rate certainly speaks to the confusion of this lifestyle of Homosexuality and by this rainbow symbol of life representing the Homosexual Community is also a Umbrella Covenant Symbol of Death and Destruction as well.

# CHAPTER IX

## Queen James

The Queen James is an official bible of the homosexual community. This is a version derived from the King James to which the King James Version is one of two public domain bible manuscripts. Many speak of the King James Version as the most holy of bible versions, but how can that be when the King James came from the original manuscript written in Hebrew being of the Old Testament. The King James was not the first westernize bible, the King James came after the Geneva Version which was written in fragment sentencing. The Roman Catholic Church began such version as well as the Catholic Church setting the standards for all denominational church body. The Catholic Church established what was called the bible society. The bible society ordered by King James was set up with 50 chosen scholars Shakespeare and Michael Angelo being lead on these manuscripts. There were reports that suggested they were lovers and they fell apart. This led Shakespeare to be the overall lead scholar on this manuscript, which in this version it was by law that no one outside the Kings Kingdom were allowed to read this bible. The problem with the King James is simple it lacks clarity, no understands shake spearing language, thee, thou and thus. You cannot give this bible tone not equipped to knowing such language. So it is easy being a public domain manuscript for the homosexual community to edit this bible. It is also comfortable for the homosexual community to use the King James manuscript to copy from because homosexual lifestyle was highly practice in the Kings castle. In the Queen James, the word effeminate is changed to morally weak and the words; "Abusers of themselves with mankind" is changed to promiscuous, because both in the Kings James Bible clearly point to the sin of sodomy.

The text puts homosexuals with others who shall not inherit the Kingdom of God. **7. I Timothy 1:10,** *"For whoremongers, for them that defile them-selves with mankind, for men stealers, for liars, for perjured persons, and if there be any other thing that is contrary to sound doctrine ; . . . "* The Queen James in this verse changed, "defile themselves with mankind to simply "defile themselves." Again, this is an attack on God's Word and the justification of the wicked and vile sin of sodomy. **8. Jude 7**, *"Even as Sodom and Gomorrha, and the cities about them in like manner, giving themselves over to fornication, and going after strange flesh, are set forth for an example, suffering the vengeance of eternal fire."* The Queen James has changed the word "strange" flesh to "nonhuman" flesh, to align the text with its change in **Genesis 19:5**. The editors has said that they chose to highlight the fact that the mad mob in Sodom raped angels, which is strange, in that it is nonhuman. But, the problem with this statement is that the men of Sodom did not know Lot's visitors were angels. God did not destroy the sodomites because of their desire for nonhumans, but for their vile affections in same sex unions long before the angels ever visited the city. The Queen James is a perversion of the Bible. It is an attempt to rewrite the Scripture, which is blasphemy. The sin of sodomy is still an abomination and always will be, and God will judge those who have corrupted His Holy Word (**Deuteronomy 23:17, I Kings 14:24; 15:12; 22:46; II Kings 23:7**). The only solution is repentance toward According to their website, queenjamesbible.com, the Queen James Bible was released in November, 2012. It is advertised as the first gay bible with a cross on the front cover in rainbow colors. The sales pitch on the website says, "You can't choose your sexuality, but you can choose Jesus. Now you can choose a Bible, too."

## Queen James

In other words, you can read the Bible and practice sodomy. Being a revision of the King James Bible to promote sexual perversion, the editors changed eight verses that deal with sodomy, that is, they add to and took away from God's Word to justify their sin.

Here is what's said by the editors:

Homosexuality was first mentioned in the Bible in 1946 in the Revised Standard Version. **There is no mention of or reference to homosexuality in any Bible prior to this — only interpretations have been made.** Anti-LGBT Bible interpretations commonly cite only eight verses in the Bible that they interpret to mean homosexuality is a sin; eight verses in a book of thousands!

**The Queen James Bible seeks to resolve interpretive ambiguity in the Bible as it pertains to homosexuality: We edited those eight verses in a way that makes homophobic interpretations impossible.**

1. **Genesis 19:5**

    **KJV:** And they called unto Lot, and said unto him, Where are the men which came in to thee this night? Bring them out unto us, that we may know them.

    **QJV:** And they called unto Lot, and said unto him, Where are the men which came in to thee this night? Bring them out unto us, that we may rape and humiliate them. (Page 21)

2. **Leviticus 18:22**

    **KJV:** Thou shalt not lie with mankind, as with womankind: it is an abomination.

**QJV:** Thou shalt not lie with mankind as with womankind in the temple of Molech: it is an abomination. (Page 75)

3. **Leviticus 20:13**

**KJV:** If a man also lie with mankind, as he lieth with a woman, both of them have committed an abomination: they shall surely be put to death; their blood shall be upon them.

**QJV:** If a man also lie with mankind in the temple of Molech, as he lieth with a woman, both of them have committed an abomination: they shall surely be put to death; their blood shall be upon them. (Page 76)

4. **Romans 1:26**

**KJV:** For this cause God gave them up unto vile affections: for even their women did change the natural use into that which is against their nature.

**QJV:** Their women did change their natural use into that which is against nature: And likewise also the men left of the natural use of the woman, burned in ritual lust, one toward another. (Page 545)

5. **Romans 1:27**

**KJV:** And likewise also the men, leaving the natural use of the woman, burned in their lust one toward another; men with men working that which is unseemly, and receiving in themselves that recompense of their error which was meet.

**QJV:** Men with men working that which is pagan and unseemly. For this cause God gave the idolaters up unto vile affections, receiving in themselves that recompense of their error which was meeting. (Page 545)

**6.** **1 Corinthians 6:9**

**KJV:** Know ye not that the unrighteous shall not inherit the kingdom of God? Be not deceived: neither fornicators, nor idolaters, nor adulterers, nor effeminate, nor abusers of themselves with mankind.

**QJV:** Know ye not that the unrighteous shall not inherit the kingdom of God? Be not deceived: neither fornicators, nor idolaters, nor adulterers, nor morally weak, nor promiscuous. (Page 554)

**1 Corinthians 6:10**

**KJV:** Nor thieves, nor covetous, nor drunkards, nor revilers, nor extortioners, shall inherit the kingdom of God.

**QJV:** Nor thieves, nor covetous, nor drunkards, nor revilers, nor extortioners, shall inherit the kingdom of God. (Page 554)

**1 Timothy 1:10**

**KJV:** For whoremongers, for them that defile themselves with mankind, for men stealers, for liars, for perjured persons, and if there be any other thing that is contrary to sound doctrine.

**QJV:** For whoremongers, for them that defile themselves, for men stealers, for liars, for perjured persons, and if there be any other thing that is contrary to sound doctrine. (Page 575)

**7.** **Jude 1:7**

**KJV:** Even as Sodom and Gomorrha, and the cities about them in like manner, giving themselves over to fornication, and going after strange flesh, are set forth for an example, suffering the vengeance of eternal fire.

**QJV:** Even as Sodom and Gomorrha, and the cities about them in like manner, giving themselves over to fornication, and going after nonhuman flesh, are set forth for an example, suffering the vengeance of eternal fire.

The bottom line is simple, the greatest response to such a perverted manuscript of scripture is in: Rev 22:19 "And if any man shall take away from the words of the book of this prophecy, God shall take away his part out of the book of life, and out of the holy city, and *from* the things which are written in this book" (KJV). This I would like to see what changes were made to this verse of scripture in the Queen James!

## A Message to the Christian

In much of the Homosexual Communities battle for rights they used a simple system to carry out their agenda. They declared Civil Rights which put them in position before the legal system to have a great and powerful leverage to influence the courts to favor their agenda. One way in doing so is to make their argument about human rights under the title of civil rights. Another way of doing so is to be sure to know who amongst the high judges are gay or lesbian and build their momentum to move their case before such judge, which would easily give them victory. The church problem is 1.) The church gave more of its opinion about this matter than the word of GOD. 2.) The church fought a battle against flesh and blood rather than spirits and principalities. 3.) The church argued the wrong point of same sex marriage and marital benefits. 4.) The church argument must be the point in which GODS word points out that the "ACTS' of a man loving another man as he would a woman is against the Kingdom of GOD period. 5.) The "ACTS" of a woman loving another woman as she would a man is against the Kingdom of GOD period.

The church cannot maintain its argument upon same sex marriages, to change the Homosexual Community wave of victorious momentum in many parts of the world, the church must get back to GOD through Christ Jesus and under the instruction of the Holy Spirit, by way of our contract we accepted upon receiving the salvation of GOD. This contract is called the "Great Commission" and this contract calls for us to preach and teach the gospel of the Kingdom of GOD through the world that one can also be saved as we are saved. And as the Bible says it best it is only when the message of the Kingdom of GOD id preached in the four corners of the earth the end of the world will come. Not an earthly disastrous moment, the Message of the Kingdom is preach in the four corners of the world. That means us "Church ", it means we as GODS Kingdom Community must teach the people to change their way of thinking and lead them to what is called repentance. Not argue your "OPINION". Amen!!!

THE KINGDOM CULTUREFELLOWSHIP MINISTRIES
&
CHRISTIAN SELF PUBLISHING CO.

THE KINGDOM CULTURE EXPLORATORY
STUDY BIBLE

THE KINGDOM ENGLISH STANDARD BIBLE

www.ingramcontent.com/pod-product-compliance
Lightning Source LLC
Chambersburg PA
CBHW021141230426
43667CB00005B/204